# THE AMERICAN STATE FAIR

## DEREK NELSON

**MOTORBOOKS**
INTERNATIONAL

## DEDICATION

For everyone who tried for a kewpie but missed.
For everyone who couldn't afford a sideshow but whose imagination was even better than the show would have been.
For everyone who knows that corn dogs, caramel popcorn, and lemonade are the perfect diet for a fairground marathon.
For every child whose carousel horse felt like Dan Patch on the home stretch.
For everyone who was too excited to sleep the night before and too tired to stay awake on the way home.

This edition published in 2004 by Motorbooks International, an imprint of MBI Publishing Company, Galtier Plaza, Suite 200, 380 Jackson Street, St. Paul, MN 55101-3885 U.S.A.

© Derek Nelson, 1999, 2003

First published in 1999 by MBI Publishing Company.

Motorbooks International titles are also available at discounts in bulk quantity for industrial or sales-promotional use. For details write to Special Sales Manager at Motorbooks International Wholesalers & Distributors, Galtier Plaza, Suite 200, 380 Jackson Street, St. Paul, MN 55101-3885 U.S.A.

ISBN 0-7603-1917-0

**On the front cover:** (Clockwise from upper left) #1: If the wild animals on display were half as dangerous as the garish posters made them appear, the feel of Dad's big hand was comforting. #2: Elephants from a circus parade decorate two of the letters on this postcard. Toward the end of their heyday in America, circus troups found fairs to be ideal venues. #3: This behemoth was the original Ferris wheel introduced to a spellbound audience at the World's Columbian Exposition in Chicago in 1893. #4: The 68 hand-carved wooden horses from this carousel, a memorable feature of the Minnesota State Fair for three-quarters of a century, were saved from the auction block by a community effort in 1988. #5: The animals took center stage at many of the nation's state fairs, including this 1909 California event featuring poultry.

**On the frontispiece:** Lavish poster art was used to advertise state fairs in the early part of the 20th century. This fine example is a poster from the 1918 California State Fair. *California History Section, California State Library*

**On the title page:** One of the longest-standing, not to mention most popular, rides at the state fair is the Ferris wheel. *J.C. Allen and Son, Inc.*

**On the back cover:** (Left) Since this talker has a microphone, he isn't leather-lunging it, a term from the days when volume was self-generated. (Right) A poster advertising the equestrian attractions at the California State Fair.

Printed in China

# CONTENTS

# ACKNOWLEDGMENTS

As always, my first and best thanks go to my wife, Mary, and my son, Nate, both veterans of an unexpected number of books, who remain willing to listen to yet another passage that may or may not be fine, and to hear yet another anecdote that may or may not be interesting. Without their patient support, my career as an author would have been shorter and much less fun.

Thanks to Kathie Swift, marketing director at the Iowa State Fair, and her staff for their hospitality and guidance as I tramped that fair's wonderful fairground in the summer of 1998. Likewise to Jeff Fites of the Marketing Department at the Indiana State Fair, for introducing me to folks and pointing out things not to miss as I logged some busy miles gawking, chatting, and eating at the Indiana fair.

John Allen of J. C. Allen and Son, Inc., took the time to meet me and share with me some of his amazing collection of photos of the Indiana fair. His helpfulness and attention to detail were crucial in shaping this book.

The staff at the Minnesota State Fair has consistently exceeded all expectations in terms of patience and helpfulness. Tracy Schlumpberger, no longer with the fair, greeted this project with enthusiasm two years ago, and numerous staff members—notably Amanda Engquist, publications supervisor (and recipient of at least two dozen phone calls of varying levels of urgency), Gale Frost, Susan Quick, and Ken Giannini, marketing support supervisor, all proved extraordinarily valuable in finding and providing information and imagery.

Lavon Shook of Columbus, Ohio, who offered a considerable amount of his time, energy, and expertise to help me include material about the Ohio State Fair

Mike Bradley and Missy Kinder at the California State Fair both worked hard to ensure that the Golden State's historic fair was adequately represented in this book with some fine photos.

Kathy Watson of the Arkansas State Fair and Cindy Fribourgh (senior account executive at Cranford Johnson Robinson Woods, an advertising and public relations firm in Little Rock) proved both friendly and resourceful in helping me obtain colorful posters from the state's fair.

Pamela Edwards, public relations and special programs coordinator, and Marlene Pearson, assistant manager, at the State Fair of West Virginia went the extra mile to photograph some of their fine collection of artifacts for me.

Jerry Wiebel, managing editor of *Country* magazine, gave me the opportunity to receive dozens of funny and touching letters from his readers, adding a human dimension to this text that would have been nearly impossible to obtain elsewhere.

The following folks also helped me ferret out obscure details, scoured the card catalogs and crowded shelves of libraries and archives, took the time to chat or write, and in general provided the grist for my literary mill. I have listed them not in the order of their contribution, but in the usual alphabetic style.

Ellen V. Alers, archivist, Maryland State Archives; Matthew Benz, reference archivist, Ohio Historical Society; Peter Boehm, Our Fair Carousel, Inc., St. Paul, Minnesota; Donaly E. Brice, supervisor, Reference Services, Texas State Library and Archives Commission; Andy Cashman, assistant general manager, and Joan Cassens, Maryland State Fair; Vicki Casteel, visual collections archivist, State Archives of Indiana; Jean Coffey, Sanoian Special Collections Library, Henry Madden Library, California State University; Gail Miller Deloach, Georgia Department of Archives and History; Bonnie Dwyer, reference librarian, Maine State Library; Philip Earl, Nevada Historical Society; Joan M. Elliott, coordinator, Ag Development, New Jersey Agricultural Society; Mrs. Bette M. Epstein, head of reference, New Jersey Archives and Records Management; Kim Frontz, Library and Archives, Arizona Historical Society; Dan Fuller, Visual Materials Archive, State Historical Society of Wisconsin; Bob Goldsack, editor, *Midway Journal*; William M Grace, reference archivist, Center for Historical Research, Kansas State Historical Society; Cathy Griffin, state documents librarian, Research Division, Arizona Department of Library, Archives, and Public Records; Kathy Harmer, Atlanta History Center; Patricia Henry, Springfield, Illinois; Dutch Holland, demolition derby promoter, El Centro, California; Randy Hooker, marketing director, Delaware State Fair; Anne Marie Ickes, reference archivist, Pennsylvania State Archives; Alan F. January, department head, Indiana State Archives; Marilyn Johnson, Nebraska State Fair; John H. Keenan, Burnsville, Minnesota; Charlotte Kennedy, Durham Agricultural Fair in Connecticut; Andy Kraushaar, reference archivist, Visual Materials Archive, State Historical Society of Wisconsin; Gary Kurutz, California State Library; Michelle Leavell, Marketing Department, Indiana State Fair; Mike Line, Special Collections and University Archives, Robert E. Kennedy Library, Cal Poly State University; Curtis Mann, Sangamon Valley Collection, Lincoln Library; Karen Mann, assistant manager of promotions and advertising, State Fair of Oklahoma, Inc.; Steve Massengill, North Carolina Department of Archives and History; Harold Miller, reference archivist, State Historical Society of Wisconsin; Bonnie J. Morgan, Photograph Archives, Montana Historical Society; Suzanne Moss, Manager, Office of Promotional Events, Illinois State Fair; Pam Nelson, Photograph Curator, Churchill County Museum and Archives, Fallon, Nevada; Steve Nielsen, reference associate, Minnesota Historical Society; Sherry Powell and Joyce Covington, special events coordinator, Florida State Fair; Stephanie Philbrick, reference assistant, Maine Historical Society; Al Regensberg, senior archivist, New Mexico State Records Center and Archives; Michael Rose, Visual Arts Department, Atlanta History Center; Ed Russo, Sangamon Valley Collection, Lincoln Library; Jill Schaller, marketing and public relations director, Ohio State Fair at the Ohio Exposition Center; Edward Skipworth, Special Collections and Archives, Rutgers University Libraries; Todd Shaffer, reference archivist, Oregon Archives Division; Brian Shovers, reference historian, Montana Historical Society; Peggy Simmons,

News Research Department Library, News and Observer Publishing Co., Raleigh, North Carolina; Edward Skipworth, Special Collections and Archives, Rutgers University Libraries; John Skold, manager, Nebraska State Fair; Jennifer Stokes, marketing and event coordinator, Alaska State Fair; Jim Sumner, curator of sports and recreation, North Carolina Department of Cultural Resources, Archives and History; Sibyl Strates Doremus, public relations director, James E. Strates Shows; Ellen L. Sulser, archives associate, State Historical Society of Iowa; Noreen Tassinari, director of marketing, Eastern State Expositions; Teresa Taylor, Special Collections and University Archives,

Robert E. Kennedy Library, Cal Poly State University; Utah State Historical Society; Richard Waldron, executive director, New Jersey Historical Commission; Patti Warren, Member Services, International Association of Fairs and Expositions; Jerry Wiebel, managing editor, *Country* magazine, and the dozens of his readers who sent me their funny and touching recollections of fairs long past but still vivid; Nancy Wiley, vice president of communications, and Candis Wheat, public relations staff, State Fair of Texas; Nancy Windisch, executive secretary, Indiana State Fair; and Lisa Wood, Ohio Historical Society. —Derek Nelson

## PREFACE

Who can forget the first visit to the fair—a magical land of sights and sounds and smells beyond the reach of teachers, bosses, worries, and chores? There's nothing quite like that strange, veritable city that rises anew year after year on the outskirts of town to fill youths with wide-eyed wonder and adults with vivid memories of their own childhoods. For many people and many generations, the fair has occupied its own special place on the calendar and in the heart.

The American state fair is a conceptual curiosity, a celebration of agriculture that is at once a fantastic departure from the discipline and labor of the farming life. Even at the earliest fairs, agricultural displays and discussions competed for space and attention with horse races, carnivals, and shows. And innovations only widened the gap. The plowing contest became the tractor pull, and the horse race led to auto and motorcycle races and automobile stunt shows. Horse and hog contests blossomed into competitions among every kind of animal and vegetable, with baking and sewing contests right alongside. Like the prizewinning livestock and produce they showcased, state fairs expanded in size and number, becoming a national institution.

Agricultural fairs reach back to biblical times and promise to stretch far into the future. My tribute to the American state fair picks up around the time of the Civil War, when many of the country's best-known and largest state fairs were first held. Before then, fairs were mostly local or countywide affairs, more serious and less entertaining. But after the Civil War, the thrill shows, contests, and pageants that became such an integral part of our fair experience appeared to enliven the event.

I've drawn the curtain on fairs during the 1950s because that decade signaled a change in their significance as the country shifted from an agricultural to an industrial and service-based economy. The farming community began to shrink after World War I—a trend that

**Butter sculptures date back to the turn of the century. Most feature cows and barnyard scenes, although sculptors sometimes chose politicians or celebrities. This heroic vision of Teddy Roosevelt was created by the Milton Dairy Company of St. Paul. Photos of the sculpture distributed by the company included this caption: "If you are a dairy farmer sell us your Cream . . . you will get a square deal and courteous treatment . . . If you . . . want ice cream, see our representative in your hometown. "** Minnesota Historical Society

accelerated after World War II. At the time of the Civil War, the vast majority of Americans supported themselves through agriculture; by 1940, only a quarter of all Americans lived on farms, and by 1980, that number was down to three of every hundred. Rural America was disappearing,

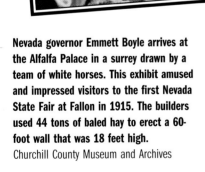

**Nevada governor Emmett Boyle arrives at the Alfalfa Palace in a surrey drawn by a team of white horses. This exhibit amused and impressed visitors to the first Nevada State Fair at Fallon in 1915. The builders used 44 tons of baled hay to erect a 60-foot wall that was 18 feet high.**
Churchill County Museum and Archives

and although fairs were thriving, the crowds in attendance were more often city or suburban dwellers who saw livestock about as often as they saw animals in zoos.

Fairs have changed with the people who have sponsored them, but tradition and innovation remain constant. In the 1860s and 1870s, fairs closed at dusk because gas lights and electricity were still decades in the future. Implements from that time, then considered revolutionary, live on in exhibits of agricultural history. By the 1950s, the Texas fair was installing a monorail, and the Indiana fair was displaying a replica of an atomic pile at an exhibit of nuclear energy. But at both fairs, the venerable Ferris wheel, invented at the turn of the century, was still a centerpiece of the midway. New meets old at the fair, and always takes something fresh from the encounter.

From a journalist's point of view, a century of state fair snapshots and anecdotes is an embarrassment of riches. Concluding with the 1950s lets me include material that older readers can remember, while concentrating on events, trends, and connections that are less familiar and more remarkable. That one-hundred years offered the public a cavalcade of exciting, odd, funny, heart-warming, startling, and amazing things. Monkeys dressed in hats and danced to minstrel music at the Ohio State Fair in 1853. Monkeys drove miniature hot rods in California in the 1950s (the first aid tent, one year, treated 10 people for monkey bites, along with the usual hundreds of stomachaches and dozens of lost children).

Fairs held butter-making contests. A dairy company presented a butter sculpture of Teddy Roosevelt, posed with his foot on a dead lion; a live lion once rode in a race car. Elsewhere, a butter sculptor carved a John Deere tractor. Fairs featured tractors when they were newfangled inventions that some farmers figured would never replace horses. Those same tractors appeared at displays of antique farm equipment 100 years later, where they evoked nostalgia for a simpler time.

Sure, fairs are corny—that's why folks love them. Where else could you see a replica of the Statue of Liberty made of ears of corn? Or the state's tallest corn stalk? Or watch contestants vie to slice off the longest apple peel? Or see a Liberty Bell made of apples?

Such attractions were irresistible. Small boys sneaked into fairs by climbing under the fence. Gypsies got kicked out through the front gate for cheating the customers.

Pretty girls wore new styles during fashion shows. Pretty girls in cooch shows wore not much at all. Pretty cows had their own events, as did fat cattle. Fat women headlined freak shows, along with wild men from Borneo.

You could see the eruption of Mount Vesuvius depicted on a huge mural. The Battle of Manila in fireworks shot high into the night sky. A daredevil shot from a cannon. A car (the Torpedobile) shot from a cannon.

Big shots gave speeches. Trick shots entertained the crowds. Suffragettes rubbed elbows with prohibitionists; bootleggers offered shots of illicit liquor. Bamboozlers thrived. Bamboo novelty canes sold like hotcakes.

Big Tex, official greeter at the Texas State Fair, was originally the world's largest Santa Claus before he became an honorary citizen of the Lone Star state. He now sports size 70 boots and a 75-gallon hat. His waist measures 284 inches, and his head is 8 feet from chin to top. In 1953 mechanics added a one-horse-power motor to his jaw so that he could move it in synch to announcements, which are, as a sign of our bilingual times, now broadcast in English and Spanish. In 1997 they rebuilt his arm so that he could wave, too.

Parched fairgoers swilled draft beer and eyed draft horses. Draftees poured into fairgrounds during four wars, turning barns into barracks. One fairground became a prisoner-of-war camp during the Civil War. At another fairground, a huge family campground has been popular for generations.

At fairs from Florida to Alaska, farmers and ranchers have shown enough livestock to fill 10,000 Noah's arks, and gardeners enough jars of fruits and vegetables to build a pyramid for a pharaoh.

You can see a display of crops that are no more: amaranth, crambe, lupine, and flax. You can see cages of pigeons with names you've never heard: Oriental Frills, Modenas, Fantails, Birmingham Rollers, Turbils, and White Kings.

You could have seen Blue Boy (the prizewinning hog in Phil Stong's novel *State Fair*), or Old Oscar (the Iowa State Fair's famous sturgeon, who spent 28 years as an attraction at the fair before dying in his tank on the last day of the fair in 1954). You can still peer up at Big Tex, the giant robot who greets people (in English and Spanish) at the Texas State Fair.

Honest Abe spoke at the Wisconsin State Fair in 1859 (he was paid $150, which included his expenses). A century later, the Kentucky State Fair held Abraham Lincoln look-alike contests.

Racers galore vied for ribbons, trophies, and loot; events featured horses, mules, camels, burros, dogs, boys, people riding on bikes or riding in wheelbarrows. Ostriches raced. At the World's Columbian Exposition in Chicago in 1893, an entrepreneur named E. R. Johnson of Fallbrook, California, did a steady business by serving omelets made from the eggs laid by his flock of 28 ostriches. At the Virginia State Fair two years ago, I ate an ostrich burger with my son.

Your chance to add to this list lies only as distantly as the next fair in your state. Until then, this book may help fill the time. I hope it will offer you, as it did me during my research, surprises, memories, and laughter.

# CHAPTER ONE

# The Calendar Was Built Around Fair Week

The jangly refrain of the carousel blends with the bleats and squawks of livestock, a minstrel show's ragtime and exotic music from a dimly lit tent of "oriental" dancers. At an exhibit of farm implements, gas engines backfire, echoed by the sharp cracks of rifles from a shooting gallery nearby.

At the top of the towering Ferris wheel—the highest point for miles around—excited riders survey the busy fairgrounds and the pastoral panorama that stretch into the distance. Along the midway, gaudy show boards depict a snake charmer, a palm reader, and a sword swallower. A lean, tanned farmer moseys over to study the new tractors, while his wife makes a beeline to the quilt display (she won a red ribbon last year). The 4-H contests start after lunch; until then, the kids try to be in five places at once, tugged back and forth by the patter of pitchmen and by the potent aromas of caramel popcorn and barbecued pork.

The scene is a state fair during the 1920s, but the decade scarcely matters. Fifty years earlier, the farmer might have scrutinized a new plow. At various times around the country, perhaps horses raced instead of autos, maybe the hoochie-coochie dancers were more like strippers. In any case, the essential elements of the fair scene remain unchanged. State fairs continue to pluck the strings of every sense, creating memories that resonate for a lifetime.

Who doesn't remember the lure of winning a gaudy prize at a game on the midway? Once the hottest reward was a chubby, rosy-cheeked kewpie doll. At other times, stuffed animals, stickpins, or newfangled fountain pens beckoned. The games seemed easy: toppling a pyramid of wooden bottles with a ball, or tossing a plastic ring over a peg. But one bottle didn't fall, even though you hit it, or the ring bounced off, even though you threw it perfectly.

The weather wasn't always perfect, either: choking clouds of dust blanketed people and livestock alike, and ankle-deep mud clogged the walkways after a late afternoon thunderstorm drenched the fairground. And usually nickels were scarce; kids had to choose between two rare treats, an ice cream cone and a cold bottle of soda pop, because they could afford just one.

It was a tough choice, but either way, the result was sweet—as are most memories of fairs. Plenty of distractions always await, making disappointments brief. The fair's annual pandemonium brings out the child in all of us, and draws us back year after year.

Americans didn't invent fairs—the Old Testament Book of Ezekiel mentions horse trading at fairs, and Europeans had a long tradition, going back to medieval times, of huge trade fairs in prominent cities. But Americans took fairs to heart and expanded them

> "The journey to the fair resembled in many respects the caravans of old. Down the dusty roads the procession moved, slowly winding its way over hills and through the valleys like a monster parade."
> —BILLBOARD, MARCH 20, 1920

**Once the central event in an agricultural society, the state fair evolved into a major event for rural as well as urban folk. Huge crowds attended the 11-day centennial of the California State Fair in 1954.** California State Fair

If the wild animals on display were half as dangerous as the garish posters made them appear, the feel of Dad's big hand was comforting. This photo was taken at the Central Iowa 4-H fair in Marshalltown, Iowa, September 1939.
Arthur Rothstein/Library of Congress, LC-USF33-3352-M4

in an unprecedented way, making them into something that served both our practical purposes, our whims, and our evolving dreams. Along the way, the state fair became a piece of bedrock Americana, with elements so familiar that they seem quintessentially domestic. The sideshow, for example, was described by *American Mercury* magazine in 1925 as "a typical American institution, as native as Sitting Bull, Cal Coolidge and reinforced underdrawers."

In the United States, a fair is something that a town or a county just ought to have. When, in 1935, 200 families from Minnesota, Michigan, and Wisconsin arrived in Alaska's Mantanuska Valley as part of a government program to provide fertile land for struggling farm families in the Midwest, one of the first things they did was to set aside space for a fairground. They held their first fair that September, with a baby contest, boxing matches, horse races, a rodeo, and lavish displays of giant cabbages, carrots, celery, onions, and peas.

The lure of the fair has been irresistible for a century and a half. Even before automobiles, as long as a state fair was within a day's travel, people came by the thousands. Schools closed. Hordes of people crossed the countryside, some walking, others riding in carriages, spring wagons, and the "one-hoss shay." If a fair was near a large city that had a station, trains brought visitors from neighboring states. Today, many folks readily travel to distant places and vacation several times a year, but these luxuries are recent developments. Before the turn of the century, from the Midwestern prairies to the deep woods of the Northeast, the week spent at the state fair once a year was the only vacation that most people had. Because it took so long to travel anywhere by wagon or carriage, fairgoers had to plan months in advance. "The calendar was built around fair week," wrote Stevenson Whitcomb Fletcher in his history of Pennsylvania farming, *Pennsylvania Agriculture and Country Life, 1840–1940* (State of Pennsylvania Historical and Museum Commission, 1955). "For 30 days before the great event, work was planned to have the wheat sowed, the corn shocked. . . . More than one farm wagon, bedded with timothy or fresh straw and carrying a cargo of wide-eyed family and home-grown food, rolled out of the barnyard soon after midnight and rumbled into the fairground at the break of day."

Once Model T Fords started rolling out of Detroit factories, families drove to the fair, where they camped for a week in canvas tents on tree-covered hills by the fairground. Better roads meant people could come from hundreds of miles away. Crowds at fairs grew to tens of thousands. Iowa journalist Phil Stong, author of *State Fair*, recorded his impressions of the era after the horse-and-buggy days for *Holiday* magazine in 1948. Going to the fair, he wrote, meant a "night journey in a truck with all the family, and with a hog or a blue-blooded bull or a few show-worthy, bad-tempered fowls crated up beside the baskets of quince jelly and angel-food cake." Whether they came on horseback, on foot, by wagon or by pickup, most of the fairgoers were farmers, bound for the event that celebrated the farming life.

Fairs have always been great places to win prizes and collect souvenirs. This plate is now displayed in Pioneer Hall at the Iowa State Fair, a historic structure packed with artifacts, exhibits, an antique flea market, and lots more. Pioneer Hall is one of the fair's few remaining buildings from the first Iowa fair in 1886.

"[A] night journey in a truck with all the family, and with a hog or a blue-blooded bull or a few show-worthy, bad-tempered fowls crated up beside the baskets of quince jelly and angel-food cake."

—PHIL STONG, WRITING IN HOLIDAY MAGAZINE, 1948.

Several generations meet to have some fun at a fair in Pie Town, New Mexico, in 1940. Pie Town was a cooperative community of homesteaders. Russell Lee/Library of Congress, LC-USF35-374

"[A]cres of booths, buildings, grandstand, race track, and oh, the merry-go-round! . . . Such a tumult of sound greeted us . . . that we were dazed and our vision blurred. Only gradually did our senses overcome tremulous excitement."

—MINNIE LEE McGE-HEE, HI! HO! COME TO THE FAIR! THE FLUVANNA FAIR, 1914–1929, FLU-VANNA COUNTY HISTORICAL SOCIETY, 1995.

Farming gave the fair its context, and the fair gave farming its most spectacular tribute. Tilling the soil was lonely; fairs were crowded. Farmers were usually miles away from their neighbors, and farther than that from what passed for a town. Going anywhere was a treat. Farm work could be dull and repetitive; fairs were exciting. Farmers were cut off from new ideas and inventions; fairs offered novelties and innovations galore. The farmers' world was a small section of the surrounding countryside; at a big state fair, they could see English bulls, European acrobats, and African lions. Interviewed in 1940, Judge James Henry Yarborough of Chester County, South Carolina, recalled the powerful impact of fairs before the turn of the century: "My companions and

Once through the ticket booth, visitors found a dozen attractions clamoring for immediate attention. This 1951 photo was made at the old Florida state fairground in Tampa. The University of Tampa is now on this site. Florida State Fair

"You can see more for 60 cents at the State Fair of Texas than anywhere else in the world."
—FAIR PRESIDENT AND DALLAS MAYOR ROBERT THORNTON, 1953.

For hard-working farm folks, fairs offered a chance to be silly and to do things just for the fun of it. Local politicians sometimes raced on camels or ostriches. Here, the secretary of the fair clowns for the crowd at Vermont's Tunbridge World's Fair in 1941. Jack Delano/Library of Congress, LC-USF-45837-D

Dallas mayor Robert Thornton put it another way in 1953: "You can see more for 60 cents at the State Fair of Texas than anywhere else in the world." True to its pitch, the fair really did offer something for everyone—the best advancements and achievements in agriculture competed for attention with the broadest range of entertainment available.

Though libraries, rural mail delivery, and radio eventually pierced the farm family's isolation, fairs remained the best way to find new tools, learn how to grow larger crops, and see better breeds of livestock. Growing food was serious business in America's agrarian economy, and fairs gave farmers an unsurpassed opportunity to meet other farmers, discuss technical problems, and share ideas. As Rollin Hart observed in *The Land That Feeds Us*, "Farming was the great engine that drove American life" from the time of the Pilgrims until as late as World War I. Crowds were drawn to anything that made this engine faster, stronger, or more versatile. The agricultural fairs of the 19th century helped change farming from a hidebound, learn-the-hard-way folk art into a modern science.

Even after the major labor-saving devices were invented and adopted during the late 1800s and early

The *Columbus Dispatch* helped usher in fair week during 1906, a year when farmers obviously enjoyed a banner year. Local newspapers have always been huge supporters of state fairs.
Ohio Expositions Commission and C. LaVon Shook

I had never been around much," he said. "We regarded a visit to Columbia and the State Fair then just about like you or I would look upon a visit to London or Berlin now."

Fairs offered an uproarious break from the quiet of the farmyard. Farm families had lives of back-breaking toil; at a fair, they could relax and have fun. The special days at the fair were everything that the daily grind of farming was not. Fairs offered community picnics, educational lectures, the circus (itself a blend of horse shows, menageries, and other traveling entertainments), peep shows and burlesque, amusement parks and carnivals. At a big state fair, these attractions merged into an extravaganza so broad a person could hardly begin to take it all in. In the early 1940s, one fair publicist calculated that if a visitor spent one minute looking at each of the fair's 57,000 exhibits, it would take 17 weeks' worth of eight-hour days to see them all. Fair president and

After the phenomenal success of the Midway Plaisance at the World Columbian Exposition in Chicago in 1893, some combination of carnival and amusement park became mandatory at fairs. Minnesota called its version the "Merry Pike" in 1913.
Minnesota Historical Society

1900s, the popularity of fairs continued. Manufacturers were always making new refinements and farmers didn't need the promise of revolutionary technologies to show up for a great time with family and friends. Though joined through time and tradition, the offerings of the midway had little connection to the implements and animals of the farm. This purely frivolous side of the fair took on a life, and an appeal, all its own.

The old market fairs and agricultural fairs had also included minor elements of entertainment or amusement. The roots of the word "fair" reach back to the Latin words *forum*, which means "marketplace," and *feriae*, "holidays." Emphasis gradually shifted from the former to the latter. People liked to learn and earn, but they also savored the chance to gasp and guffaw. The preparations for fairs, along with the daily lives of the farmers who participated in them, showed that Americans have a profound capacity for hard work. The explosive growth of the fair midway revealed our equally strong penchant for play, for showing off our muscles or our marksmanship, for staggering around in fun houses, for getting dizzy on mechanical rides that turn us upside down. Fairs developed a frivolous, spectacular side that sometimes demanded center stage.

For city folks, commercial entertainment was already becoming inexpensive and accessible, and thus had lost some of its original impact. For farmers still out of the mainstream of modern culture, however, the amusements offered at fairs possessed an extraordinary appeal. Fairgoers gawked at mules diving off towers

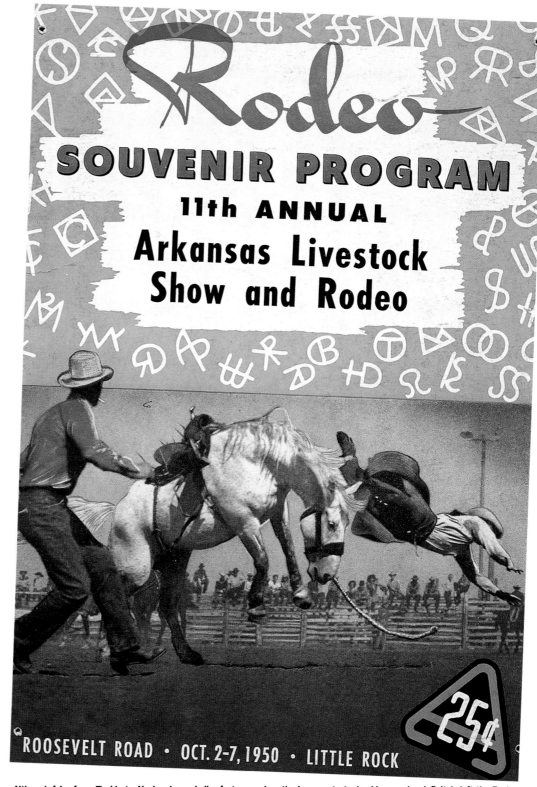

Although fairs from Florida to Alaska share similar features, when the broncs start a-bucking, you've definitely left the East.
Arkansas State Fair

During the 1950s, a new generation of celebrities from Hollywood and television drew huge crowds to their shows at fairs across the country. At the 1956 Ohio fair, for example, Hopalong Cassidy, Lassie, and Roy Rogers and Dale Evans appeared before the grandstand; the next year, Ricky Nelson, Rin-Tin-Tin, and Tennessee Ernie Ford did shows. Arkansas State Fair

"We regarded a visit to Columbia and the State Fair then just about like you or I would look upon a visit to London or Berlin now."

—JUDGE JAMES HENRY YARBOROUGH, CHESTER COUNTY, SOUTH CAROLINA, 1940.

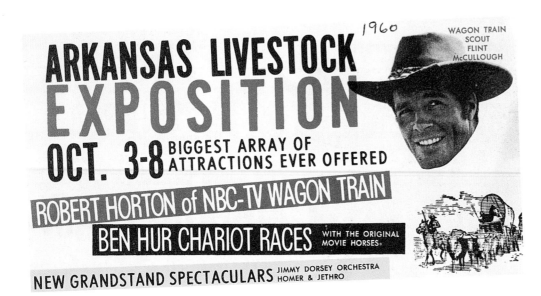

A collage of artifacts from West Virginia's state fair archives. Note the judge's badge. The clown riding the bull may have been part of a midway show that year. Eamswood Communications, Inc., for the State Fair of West Virginia

In 1925 the Ohio State Fair was held in Columbus. In recognition of the fair's upcoming Diamond Jubilee (the 75th fair), the fair board sponsored a slogan contest. The winning slogan, which earned the author a new Buick, appears at the bottom. Ohio Expositions Commission and C. LaVon Shook

This Indiana State Fair poster from 1885 sums up the state fair's traditional focus on the old and the new: history is represented by the 1816 cabin at center, farming by bucolic scenes of plenty, and progress in the form of modern transportation.

into tanks of water. They lined up for a chance to swing a huge mallet, ring a bell, and win a cigar. They gaped as steely-eyed gents floated into the sky in wicker baskets attached to risky-looking balloons. In ensuing decades, similar daredevils walked the flimsy wings of biplanes, and rode cars blasted out of huge cannons.

As a vacation, the fair was a whopper. In her reminiscence about the Fluvanna, Virginia, fair in the 1920s, historian Minnie Lee McGehee called it a "fairyland," with "acres of booths, buildings, grandstand, racetrack, and oh, the merry-go-round! Such a tumult of sound greeted us . . . that we were dazed and our vision blurred. Only gradually did our senses overcome tremu-

lous excitement. . . ." She did not exaggerate when she called the annual fair "the greatest thrill of childhood and the highlight of the year for the whole family."

America's rapidly expanding boundaries and population created an extraordinarily fertile ground for the growth of fairs, a growth in number, size, and diversity that has continued virtually unchecked, and that has weathered the effects of wars, the Depression, and the sweeping social changes that radically transformed American life in the 20th century. By the mid-1950s, more than 2,000 state, regional, and county fairs

Serious checker players vie for the Iowa state championship on the veranda of the fair's administration building in 1952. Today, the shady porch is furnished with chairs and benches so that foot-weary fairgoers can take a welcome break from the hubbub.

Margaret Maple of Howard County, Indiana, looks well-pleased with the judge's decision in the canning contest at the 1941 Indiana fair. J. C. Allen and Son, Inc.

exhibits, and trials of draught horses, the same sideshows, fakirs, [and] freaks." An article in *Popular Mechanics* magazine from 1939 observed that audiences—which would number some 50 million at 2,500 outdoor fairs and celebrations that season—were becoming blasé: "so jaded [is] the modern thrill-seekers' taste that daredevils almost have to destroy themselves to win favor . . . the so-called death-defying feats of the past would rate no more than a collective yawn today."

Other critics asserted that fairs were losing touch with their true roots in the soil. One historian opined that the agricultural fair, established to serve farmers, had degenerated into a "commercialized and urbanized amusement park." Some farmers stopped attending. Commentators such as Charles Belmont Davis, writing in *Collier's*, observed that it would be nice if "the visiting farmer will take away from the fairs something more useful than a headache, a pair of imitation diamond cuff buttons, and a vision of a lady in tights doing stunts on the flying trapeze."

The criticism went beyond boredom, to allegations of illegal and scandalous conduct. Race tracks and the boisterous midway quickly became sites of skirmishes between purity and profit, between the serious and the silly. The spectacular popularity of horse racing (and the attendant problem of gambling) drew a steady steam of protest. Midways grew increasingly controversial. Naive

opened their gates every year, drawing 85 million people (six times the total gate of major league baseball games). The Texas State Fair attracted more than 2 million; the fairs in California, Michigan, Iowa, Wisconsin, and Indiana all drew between 500,000 and 1million. By the mid-1980s, 125 million Americans attended agricultural fairs every year.

The reason for this popularity is that, throughout their sprawling, tumultuous history, state fairs have always reflected the basic elements of the national character: the strengths and weaknesses, the common sense and faddishness, the unities and discords that have long marked Americans' unique development as a people. Describing Iowa's annual extravaganza (inspiration for Phil Stong's famous novel and the ensuing films and musical), a *Time* magazine writer understood this fact: "the people who go to the Fair are Iowa itself, in all its friendliness, power, vulgarity, and genius."

The vast growth and appeal of fairs have not come in the absence of critics, only in spite of them. Like other long-lived institutions, fairs have endured the criticisms and changing tastes of the public. As early as the 1860s, some farmers denounced plows you could ride on as impractical or cruel to horses. By the turn of the century, critics complained about repetition, grumbling that fairs lacked imagination—that they all had "the same horse trots, ball games, bicycle races, livestock

fairgoers got gypped by crooked "carnies," the often derisive term for the game attendants. Wives, mothers, and ministers were shocked to learn that female entertainers were peeling off their clothes to reveal much more than a glimpse of stocking. Before Prohibition, members of the Women's Christian Temperance Union complained that rowdy fairgoers smuggled in pints of bourbon in hip flasks without being instantly spotted and evicted.

Complaints and scandal brought publicity fairs would rather have avoided, but most people took it in stride. Whenever huge crowds gather in pursuit of commercial entertainment, the cheats and the vultures eventually show up. Fairs were no different. The most egregious offenses for gambling or obscenity might have closed down a booth or event, but the image of the fair took on little tarnish. In the American tradition, fairgoers don't like to be cheated, but they don't like to be told what's good for them, either. Fairs proved too big, too diverse, and too popular to be undone by a few dissenters. Fairs promise something—not everything—for everyone, and it never takes much imagination or effort to find an item of interest if the one before you falls short.

Whether your first fair was a week ago, or decades ago, this book will spark vivid memories. Newcomers to the event will discover what made fairs loom so large in the annual calendars of their parents and grandparents. Underlying all the things that still seem surprising and

novel, and all the things that now seem quaint and outmoded, is a powerful, unifying tradition. The people who flocked to state fairs in 1860 to watch a plowing contest; or in 1914 to see Lincoln Beachey fly his biplane past the grandstand a mere 12 inches off the ground, steering with his knees; or in 1950 to see the Congress of Oddities freak show, really weren't much different from people today.

# CHAPTER TWO

# The Ultimate Fulfillment of Agrarian Aspirations

The fair began with the farmer celebrating the land and its bounty. Raising the biggest and best crops or livestock benefited the farmer, but it also enlightened and inspired other farmers seeking to improve their own yields. The competition not only improved methods, but led to the introduction of new species to American agriculture. Simple contests among a few entrants burgeoned into massive competitions, covering the breadth of farming's plant and animal species and adding judges, the 4-H club, and excited and knowledgeable crowds.

The creation of the American agricultural fair is usually credited to Elkanah Watson, a wealthy Massachusetts farmer and businessman. The event involved the display of only two of his sheep. What made them fascinating was the rarity of the breed, which had only recently been imported by the American minister to Portugal, Colonel David Humphreys. Watson described the event this way: "In the Fall of 1807 I procured the first pair of Merino sheep that had appeared in Berkshire. . . . I was induced to fortify an exhibition under the great elm tree in the public square in Pittsfield of these two sheep on a certain day. Many farmers and even women were excited by curiosity to attend my humble exhibition. . . . The farmers present responded to my remarks with approbation. We became acquainted, and from that day to the present, agricultural societies, cattle shows, and all in connection therewith have predominated in my mind."

To attract attention, Watson had clanged an old ship's bell with a piece of iron. His interest in showing the sheep was more than scientific. He owned woolen mills and wanted the local farmers to raise Merinos because the wool

> "The foundation of our wealth and progress and attainment is agriculture. Upon it, all depends. . . . Its prosperity means national prosperity; its impairment, national distress."
>
> —INDIANA GOVERNOR J. FRANK HANLY, DEDICATING THE INDIANA FAIRGROUND'S NEW LIVESTOCK PAVILION, 1905

was better. The fleece from a Merino could weigh up to eight pounds, compared to just three or four pounds for a domestic sheep of the time.

Watson founded what became known as the "Berkshire system" of agricultural societies, named after the county in Massachusetts where he organized the first one in 1811. By 1857, there were 95 such societies in New England. The system spread into Indiana and Illinois, then farther south, and became an important sponsor of fairs.

Like Watson's sheep, many of the animal breeds now shown at fairs were brought to the United States from other countries. Domestic cattle, for example, were often skinny, so farmers looked abroad. Herefords came from England in the 1870s. Connecticut got its first Jersey from the Channel Islands in 1846, and 30 of Maine's first Jerseys appeared at the Maine State Fair in 1860. The foreign origins of many common breeds are apparent from their names: Durham bulls; Leicester, Southdown, and Cotswold sheep; Shanghai, Chittagong, and Brahmaputra chickens. Angus cattle arrived from Scotland in 1873. Poland Chinas, however, as all swine fanciers know, weren't from Poland or China (the breed was developed in Ohio in 1872).

Neta Lou Anderson of New Augusta, Indiana, entered two pens of chickens in the 4-H club show at the Indiana State Fair, and won a pair of blue ribbons. She holds a Rhode Island Red and a Buff Rock hen. J. C. Allen and Son, Inc.

**The animals took center stage at many of the nation's state fairs, including this 1909 California event featuring poultry.** California History Section, California State Library

In the early days, purebred livestock was so rare that most farmers could see them only at a large fair. A typical experience was recorded in 1867 when a group of Iowa farmers chipped in $10 each to buy a purebred bull to improve their stock. The problem was, they didn't know where to get one. They talked to the keeper of the livery stable at the county seat, who told them about a breeder who had a farm 100 miles away. He'd met him at the state fair.

Raising better animals improved farmers' lives. New techniques for raising and breeding animals also increased competition at state fairs. Prize animals brought money and recognition to their owners, making proper care of the animals critical. The animals' owners and tenders were under great pressure to make the contestants as appealing as possible. Judges felt the pressure, too, for their votes meant validation for some, disappointment for others—and often criticism for themselves.

The livestock competitions at the big state fairs were nothing short of intense. Six hundred railroad cars of livestock rolled into large Midwestern state fairs in the 1920s. In the 1930s, Iowa State Fair cattle shows filled six of the largest buildings on the fairground, packing in 6,000 heads of cattle from 23 states. The fair launched the festivities and events with a huge parade of livestock. The imposing splendor of this event was captured by Donald Grant in the *Christian Science Monitor* in 1937: "Nowhere, except at the Iowa State Fair . . . can Iowans witness that triumphant dramatiza-

**Livestock parade at the old California state fairground on Stockton Boulevard in Sacramento.** California State Fair

69. STATE FAIR PARK, MILWAUKEE, WIS.

Exhibitors of livestock and crops displayed their achievements in proud exposition buildings such as these at the Wisconsin fairground. Glenwood Sadler of Grand Rapids, Michigan, received this postcard in January 1919.

tion of farm husbandry—the livestock parade. The marching line of preened and beribboned horses, cattle, sheep and hogs—prize winners among 6,000 heads of livestock—is for many an Iowan the ultimate fulfillment of agrarian aspirations."

When the judging began, professional breeders discovered if their investments and state-of-the-art techniques would earn awards, thereby increasing the value of their herds and their own reputations. They spent all summer making a circuit of state fairs with their champions, competing not just for pride but for profit (by the 1950s, a champion steer might be worth $40,000—400 times that of a regular steer). Feed companies sometimes maintained huge herds, entering the best in fairs to advertise their products. Top dollar brought out the best animals in the country and attracted attention far beyond the farming community. Writer E. B. White, discussing a fair in Maine, remarked in the *New Yorker* in 1957: "I would rather have a ringside seat at a cattle sale than a box at the opera. . . ."

As intently as the professionals, young members of 4-H clubs waited to discover if their long months of caring

The Maryland State Fair doled out exceptionally nice ribbons for winners at fairs past. Current staff members have scoured local antique stores to collect some of the fair's memorabilia.
Maryland State Fair

This wholesome lass had her day in the sun at Colorado's Delta County Fair in October 1940. Russell Lee/Library of Congress, LC-USF35-253

PREMIUM LIST

ELEVENTH ANNUAL EXHIBITION
of the

GREENBRIER VALLEY
FAIR

Lewisburg-Ronceverte
West Virginia

‡‡‡‡‡‡‡‡‡‡‡‡

AUGUST 31, SEPTEMBER 1, 2, 3, 4,
1931

The illustration on this 1931 premium list from the State Fair of West Virginia suggests that local folks were interested in horses. This fair, formerly called the Greenbrier County Agricultural Exhibition, has been at Fairlea near Lewisburg since the late 1800s. In 1858 Robert E. Lee's famous horse, Traveler, was shown at the fair as a yearling.
Eamswood Communications, Inc., for the State Fair of West Virginia

for their animals—the predawn feedings, the stalls or cages that always needed cleaning, the careful grooming—had paid off. Although in terms of dollars their investments were usually small, their expenditures of time and energy were lavish, and their dreams of a blue ribbon as unwavering as any dream at the fair.

Even when someone's animal fell out of the competition in an early round, the owner was curious to see the eventual winner, with a view toward improving his or her own showing the next year. In the bleachers, parents and spectators often had lots of experience with livestock and plenty of strong opinions about which animal was superior. They arrived early, got good seats, and carefully formed their own ideas about which Alderney or Durham deserved the ribbon.

At the Iowa fair in the 1920s, journalist Phil Stong wrote in an article in *Reader's Digest* that when the horses went on display, the show building was "pack-jammed every evening with thousands of Uncle Henrys and Aunt Mamies from the vicinity of What Cheer or Keosauqua. . . ." When the official verdict differed from their own, they questioned the qualifications of the judges and let anyone nearby know what the correct decision should have been.

Way back in 1854, the poultry judges at the first Iowa State Fair studied what the entry guide listed as "Shanghais, Dorkings, Polands, Chittigongs, Brahmapootras." According to one account, the judges were "as much a curiosity as the Shanghais themselves. The judge was as grave as though he were amongst his peers in the senate, the chief justice as dignified as though he was at the head of the supreme bench of the state."

At many 19th-century fairs, stallions, brood mares, and colts were the focus because horses were so valuable for both work and transportation. Judging horse flesh was a critical skill. When Brigham Young won a prize for celery at the Utah State Fair in 1856, you can bet that he was much prouder of the $25 first prize he won for the best stallion.

What caught the eyes of judges and savvy fairgoers? What made one animal a prize winner and another an also-ran? The animal's bloodline was an obvious factor, but appearances counted just as much, and through the years contestants developed a bag of tricks to make their animals stand out.

Cattle got early morning baths, then owners smoothed rough spots on the animal's coat, ears, and tail with clippers. Next the owner might trim the hooves with large pincers, and work on the horns with a rasp and sandpaper, then polish them to make them shiny. Shoe polish worked wonders on scuffed hooves. After the invention of the electric blow dryer, horse owners had a perfect tool for fluffing out their animals' manes, if they decided not to braid them.

Sheep were touched up with blocking shears to make them shapely and smooth. Chester White pigs got a dusting with talcum powder; for the black bristles of spotted Poland Chinas, lampblack (a pigment made from soot) worked wonders.

Some fairgoers have a favorite animal. In his *Reader's Digest* article, Stong wrote: "Give me pigs! Give me a pig somewhat heavier than a Thoroughbred stallion, a pig living a life of the most devoted selfishness

"Nowhere, except at the Iowa State Fair . . . can Iowans witness that triumphant dramatization of farm husbandry—the livestock parade. The marching line of preened and beribboned horses, cattle, sheep and hogs—prize winners among 6,000 heads of livestock—is for many an Iowan the ultimate fulfillment of agrarian aspirations."
—DONALD GRANT, CHRISTIAN SCIENCE MONITOR, SEPTEMBER 1937.

and sensuality. . . ." Stong was a fan of the whole pig, including the myriad products, both scrumptious and useful, that attend the pig's demise: hams, chops, brain cheese, pickled knuckles, sausages, bacon, and hot dogs. Stong also liked the fact that pigs had a pugnacious nature. The show building for swine at the Iowa State Fair was the scene of what he called "the best fights I have ever seen," due to the fact that all boars seemed to detest all other boars. Owners, equipped with wooden shields and whips, did their best to keep the portly glad-iators in line, but with mixed success. "The fights are not encouraged except from the grandstand," Stong noted.

Massive hogs always drew a crowd at livestock exhibits. The first Minnesota State Fair, in 1860, featured what one account described as an "exhibit which attracted much admiration, and even wonder": a 640-pound Chester White barrow, sold after the fair to a St. Paul butcher for nine cents a pound. It was the largest hog ever raised in Minnesota up to that time, and folks were mighty interested in such things.

The raising of champion swine became increasingly scientific through the years, due to technical advances in the field. One of the contestants at the Minnesota State Fair in 1953, a young woman named Margaret Juhl, had recently earned a college degree in home economics, an accomplishment that apparently helped her devise menus for livestock as well as people. Helping her father raise

"The judge was as grave as though he were amongst his peers in the senate, the chief justice as dignified as though he was at the head of the supreme bench of the state."
—IOWA STATE FAIRGOER, DESCRIBING A POULTRY JUDGE, 1854.

Poultry judges confer at the 1932 Indiana State Fair. Left to right: Judge L. J. Demberger of Stew-artsville, Indiana; county agent A. V. Keesling, tying the ribbons; and O. E. Felton, Fairmount, who was in charge of the Poultry Building, keeping records. Keesling wears a 4-H cap.

swine, Juhl told reporters that their purebred hogs were "fed rations as scientifically prepared as today's canned and packaged baby food. . . . We take just as much care in feed-ing our Duroc Jerseys as the most progressive mothers do in feeding their children." The menu: coarse-ground oats and corn, 40 percent protein feed (consisting of soybean oil, linseed oil meal, wheat shorts, antibiotics, and vitamin B-12), and condensed buttermilk just before the fair.

Margaret and her cousin had each won blue ribbons with swine entered in the 1951 fair. By then it was a fam-ily tradition. In 1919, her father had first exhibited the Durocs at the fair, and since then, hogs raised by the Juhl family had won 14 grand championships. When she was a child, Margaret had earned $1,400 for a litter of eight pigs in a county 4-H contest.

Horses have been a featured attraction at the California State Fair since the state's inaugural fair in 1854, when citizens entered their favorite steed into such cat-egories as "Best Imported Stallion," "Best American Stallion," and "Best Cart Horse." In the 1930s, the California State Fair Horse Show was a prestigious event on the premier circuit, drawing top riders and horses from throughout the West.
California State Fair

Although livestock competition was supposed to be among animals of the same breed, farmers and judges sometimes branched off into larger questions, making value judgments about the qualities of various breeds. Surveying types of pigs in 1855, for example, Indiana farmer Lewis Bollman (a member of the state board of agriculture) cast a vote for the Poland China. He appreciated the fact that where common pigs tore up pastures as they rooted around, "the Polands graze more sensibly." Furthermore, he added, they don't "put up their bristles and dash off with a booh! booh! when the owner comes near, but run to meet him as gentle as pet sheep."

The following year, at the 1856 Ohio State Fair, beef judges stirred controversy by pronouncing "the whole

"That night the hog pavilion became very quiet. The tenseness of the atmosphere was gone. The hogs grunted peacefully as they slept."

—CECIL BARGER, FROM "MUCH ADO ABOUT PIGS," ATLANTIC MONTHLY, 1939.

"[G]ive me pigs! Give me a pig somewhat heavier than a Thoroughbred stallion, a pig living a life of the most devoted self-ishness and sensuality."

—PHIL STONG, READER'S DIGEST, 1920S.

Farm kids often traveled a significant distance to the fair, and ended up staying right on the premises. Library of Congress

During lean times, farm folks were fascinated by fatness. Jolly Jumbo no doubt had a human counterpart in the freak show. This photo was taken at the Shelby County Fair in Shelbyville, Kentucky, in August 1940. Marion Post Wolcott/Library of Congress, LC-USF-30977-M3

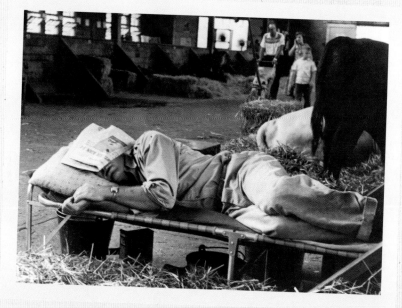

The cheapest and most convenient accommodations at any fair were right there in the livestock barn. This cowboy, as did most of his counterparts, bedded down at the San Angelo fat stock show in Texas, March 1940. Russell Lee/Library of Congress, LC-USF34-35484-D

## *The Care and Feeding of* CHAMPION HOGS

In a 1939 article in the Atlantic Monthly entitled "Much Ado About Pigs," contestant Cecil Barger recounted his annual fair ritual. He slept, partly dressed, on a cot by the hog pens; it was cheap, convenient, and allowed him to keep an eye on his prize Chester Whites. He fed them early, because they got sluggish when they were full of food, and the judges liked the animals to be alert. The timing of this meal was crucial, because after hogs fully digest their breakfasts, their sides become leaner.

Barger had already bathed them several times during the days before the judging, so their hair would be white and their skin pink; he bedded them down on clean straw. He clipped the hair around each hog's head, ears, neck, and tail. Next, he trimmed their hooves so that they would stand up on their toes, which in turn made their pasterns look stronger.

He knew what the judges were looking for in a hog: a broad back that carried evenly to the hindquarters; well-filled hams; bright, prominent eyes; and straight, well-set legs. Barger was confident that his lot looked fine, but he ran into a problem with his junior gilt. Hot and tired, the pig wanted to go back to the pen, expressing his displeasure by squealing and running up and down the fence.

Barger worried about the temperature; it made pigs droopy and sluggish, serious flaws as far as judges were concerned. Heat plagued livestock owners. It was common to see the owners of bulls, for instance, sponging the faces of their animals, oblivious to the sweat pouring down their own faces (today, owners aim large mechanical mist-makers or fans with water dripped onto their blades at their prize livestock). In the old days, as a last resort, hog owners sprinkled their animals with watering cans as the animals lay panting on the dirt or concrete floor. For some animals the battle with heat was a mortal struggle. At a Midwestern fair in 1947, a Berkshire boar valued at $5,000 got overheated and dropped dead while walking back to its stall after winning a blue ribbon.

Barger had more than the heat to worry about. His junior boar attacked another male pig, stirred up, no doubt, by the presence of certain lovely female pigs nearby. The boar's hair bristled, his ears pricked up, and the battle was on. Barger and the other owner shoved a gate panel between the two combatants.

One of Barger's pigs achieved glory that year, earning what Barger called "the coveted purple rosette ribbon" in the senior championship class. The ribbon-winner just missed becoming the grand champion boar of the show, however, losing out to a younger hog who was "livelier and had more strut."

race of Herefords inferior to Shorthorns." (Judges became more qualified and impartial with the professional development of college professors, agricultural teachers and extension agents.) Some breeds were perennial contenders, while others, with time, faded from competition. A cattle breed imported in the 1780s, the Milking Shorthorn, quickly became popular as an equally good source of both beef and milk. By the 1950s, however, fans of this breed had become somewhat defensive. Interviewed before the Minnesota State Fair in 1953, farmer Vern Immer described it as "the poor man's cow, the dirt farmer's cow." By then, Holsteins, Jerseys, and Guernseys had become the "big three" in Minnesota. The impact of the Milking Shorthorn, however, was clearly recalled by another farmer, whose grandfather had introduced the breed to what was then "the Northwest" in 1885. He had brought 50 bulls and a dozen cows from Scotland, distributing the bulls across the state. "That was a long time ago," said the fair's cattle superintendent, "but you'll still

The first Minnesota State Fair, in 1860, featured what one account described as an "exhibit which attracted much admiration, and even wonder": a 640-pound Chester White barrow, sold after the fair to a St. Paul butcher for nine cents a pound. It was the largest hog ever raised in Minnesota up to that time, and folks were mighty interested in such things.

This bulbous sow obviously had what it takes at the Minnesota State Fair. Photographers never minded photographing the winners in these categories: a handful of feed on the ground always kept the subject happy.
Minnesota State Fair

see pictures of those animals hanging in banks in western Minnesota, the Dakotas and Montana."

Breeds hold their own nostalgia. At the Oregon State Fair in 1959, Sen. Wayne Morse asked the fair commission to allow Devon cattle, a breed that had never been shown at the fair. Devons, according to some accounts, had been the first cattle brought to the American colonies by the Pilgrims in the 1620s. "Many of the covered wagons which went across the plains were pulled by Devon oxen," Morse explained.

Most of the prominent animals at large fairs were the familiar farmyard types, but a Noah's ark of others were also on display. Fairs at the turn of the century often had beekeeping exhibits. Some fairs opened categories for pets of all kinds. The 1934 Minnesota fair had some 3,000 birds on display and in competition, including chickens, geese, and a dozen

kinds of turkeys. The pigeon show at the Nebraska State Fair in 1951 drew pigeon fanciers from Nebraska, Colorado, Iowa, and Kansas, who brought along more than 600 birds. The names are evocative, particularly for folks who have only seen gray pigeons in urban parks: White Kings, Carneaui, Oriental Frills, Modenas, Fantails, Hungarians, African Owls, Birmingham Rollers, Turbils.

While most competitions focused primarily on an animal's size or appearance, other contests measured power. Premiums such as cash or a trophy were awarded for the best yoke of oxen or the best span of mules. Looking for the hardest working and strongest animals, the 1869 Illinois State Fair displayed a 1,900-pound draft horse, imported from England, which drew huge crowds. Within a few years, Norman draft horses weighing 2,300 pounds appeared at fairs.

These animals looked powerful. Just how strong were they? To answer this question, 1920s fairs in the Midwest and Northeast began holding draft horse pulls.

F. A. Bates, then a well-known breeder of Herefords from Broken Bow, Nebraska, bought this grand champion bull for $6,900 at a Nebraska State Fair. His grandson, Dickie Towns, holds the halter.
Nebraska State Fair

Guernseys get cover billing on this program from Virginia's 1969 state fair. These medium-sized dairy cattle got their name from the second largest of the Channel Islands of the United Kingdom, from which they were exported to America. Their dairy cousins, the Jerseys, got their name the same way. State Fair of Virginia

Many state fairs began as small, annual events sponsored by local or state agricultural societies, which flourished toward the end of the 19th century. After the Civil War, there were more than 1,200 state, district, county, and township agricultural societies, and many held fairs. The Maryland fair's official title in 1931 records this genesis.
Maryland State Fair

Charles Brown, 4-H member from Battle Ground, Indiana, poses with his grand champion fat wethers (castrated male sheep) in the open class at the 1930 Indiana State Fair. Brown was selected as the outstanding 4-H club boy in the United States, and won the Sir Thomas Lipton trophy for his many winning entries at local, state, and national fairs and shows, and his leadership and guidance of younger 4-H members. Brown had developed his own flock of purebred Shropshire sheep. J. C. Allen and Son, Inc.

The Waukee Wideawakes of Dallas County, Iowa, work their float for the parade at the 1920 Iowa State Fair. Many 4-H clubs sported upbeat names, such as the Ever-Readies, Bustlers, and Full-O-Pep. Iowa State Fair, Des Moines

Sometimes the horses would pull huge stones in a special sled. Another arrangement was to have them pull against a machine (usually mounted in the back of a truck) that measured the force they applied. The horses wore heavy collars and a complex arrangement of harnesses, chains, and straps. Photos often show that the truck had chains wrapped around the rear tires so the horses wouldn't drag it away. Sometimes the teamster "drove" the horses from a seat in the back of the truck.

An important group that added huge numbers of devoted entrants to the competitions over the years was the 4-H club, whose members flocked to state fairs in ever-increasing amounts. Although adult male farmers ran the early agricultural fairs primarily for themselves, opportunities for boys and girls gradually appeared. By 1904, a "junior club," which became the 4-H in 1912, grew corn to exhibit at the fair. From that point, the presence of the 4-H grew phenomenally. In the late 1920s in Indiana, more than 20,000 boys and girls were involved

"Many farmers and even women were excited by curiosity to attend my humble exhibition. . . ."

—ELKANAH WATSON, MASSACHUSETTS FARMER AND BUSINESSMAN, ABOUT 1810.

A 4-H member prepares for the finals in the livestock judging contest at the 1937 Iowa State Fair. He was one of 3,000 4-Hers from 99 counties to attend the 8-day fair that year, exhibiting colts, pigs, baby steers, heifers, and sheep.
Iowa State Fair–Des Moines

A winner congratulating his entry? Or an animal that just looked like it needed a hug? Nebraska State Fair

Judges typically awarded 40 points for the best animal, 15 points for the animal that gained the most weight as a daily average, 25 points for the cheapest cost of production, and 20 points for the best-kept record.

In Ohio, 4-H entries in the state fair began with baby beef shows in 1916, with similar explosions in numbers. In 1924, the organizers of the Wisconsin State Fair built a special camp on the fairground strictly

Although fairs began as events staged by and for farmers, they welcomed folks who were less familiar with livestock. Within a single century, America's population was transformed from 97 percent rural to 97 percent urban or suburban. Where fairs used to educate farmers, they now teach city dwellers where food comes from. Fairs may have been the original petting zoos. Nebraska State Fair

in 4-H club work. For the 1936 fair, 4-H members from 85 counties grew, raised, or made 3,277 exhibits.

The founder of 4-H club work at the Minnesota State Fair once recalled that in 1913, club exhibits at the fair were limited to corn samples. Canning and garden products were added the next year. By 1953, the 4-H contingent was huge; publicists calculated that 4-H members chowed down on two tons of potatoes and drank 19,000 half-pints of milk as part of the 20,000 meals they ate at that year's fair.

South Dakota held its first Boys State Fair Camp in 1915, with participants selected on the basis of their skill in growing corn and potatoes, and in judging crops and livestock. Formal 4-H clubs took over in 1919, entering about 100 exhibits in the fair. Within 20 years, state fair 4-H participants would number in the thousands, and their exhibits would top 10,000.

For livestock contests, the 4-H club emphasized the educational aspects of raising and caring for show animals.

"We take just as much care in feeding our Duroc Jerseys as the most progressive mothers do in feeding their children."

—MARGARET JUHL,
MINNESOTA STATE

California Governor Earl Warren presents a livestock award at the 1954 state fair. Such events—with huge, friendly crowds—are a natural venue for politicians.
California State Fair

At early fairs, volunteers created elaborate displays that were works of art in themselves, apart from whatever crop they exhibited. This fruit display graced the Utah State Fair in 1910.

for 4-H club members. A decade later, the New York State Fair built a $100,000 4-H livestock pavilion. Minnesota counted 50,000 4-H participants at the county and district level in 1941, of which 3,000 went on to the state fair. Their importance to the fair was evidenced by the building of a huge white dormitory specifically for 4-H members, equipped with 200 triple-decker bunks. In 1954, 23,000 4-H girls took part in Iowa 4-H programs, and 800 brought exhibits to the fair. That year, 100,000 members of state 4-H, Future Farmers of America, and Future Homemakers of America converged on the Texas State Fair.

Statistics and projects such as these were tangible recognition of the growing size and importance of 4-H participation. The 4-H club and the state fair seemed a match made in heaven, with shared values and interests. Club members worked all year long at the kind of things that fairs rewarded with ribbons and recognition.

The Clay County Fair in Spencer, Iowa, in September 1949, was typical of smaller, local fairs (except that *Life* magazine dispatched a photographer and a writer that year). The county had 33 4-H clubs for young people aged 10–20; 600 members took part in the county fair, with about 100 of the boys staying in a dormitory at the fairground. Their typical outfit, at least according to the magazine photos, included blue jeans and cotton shirts. The girls were more distinctive, togged out in

homemade uniforms with green and white stripes. The kids camped, played, soaked up the sights and sounds and, in general, had a good time. Some of the older boys took part in a "judging contest" to test how they'd rate various animals.

Many of the 4-H'ers raised cattle, which they'd bought the previous fall as feeder calves raised out West,

then carefully fattened on corn, barley, and oats. Some kids raised sheep. Dramatic photos in the magazine showed both kinds of animals escaping, with their exasperated owners in hot pursuit. The animals weren't used to being poked and prodded by judges, and some were more skittish than others. Animals that got loose might get dirty, or, worse yet, miss their turn in the judging ring, which would be disastrous. Once the contest began, according to the *Life* writer, the 4-H members "invested their section of the fair with an air of anxiety that turned almost to anguish at the crucial moments of judging and selling." It was, he wrote, "a deadly serious climax to a year of hard work."

One girl named her calf "Folly," because it cost her $316 to raise, but sold for just $314. A photo shows another girl with a 1,115-pound Hereford named Prince Pat that proved more lucrative; she calculated that it cost about $200 to buy and feed Prince Pat, who netted $356 at the sale. All in all, 403 cattle and 257 pigs were sold to meat packers on the last day of the fair. Some of the children looked forlorn as their animals were auctioned off. Tears trickled down more than a few freckled cheeks as the young farmers trudged away from barns or corrals, dragging empty halters in the dust.

Pigs and cattle weren't pets, after all; affectionate attachment was misplaced for animals that had appointments with a slaughterhouse. Best to adopt the down-to-earth attitude displayed by 16-year-old Faye Eileen Mugge, who had won the baby beef grand championship at the Iowa State Fair in 1953 with a steer called "Shorty." Chatting with a Des Moines reporter as she readied her entry for the 1954 fair, she observed, "I'm getting Shorty's hide as a rug." A hotel had bought the steer and was having the hide tanned for her. "Real nice of them, wasn't it?" she asked.

Any notes of disappointment and sadness were minor themes in the state fair's annual symphony. Making it to the fair was honor enough, since some breeds required the owner to win at a county fair.

Participation by 4-H clubs skyrocketed through the 1940s and 1950s; prizes and recognition grew apace. In the 1950s, the grand champion might fetch more than $1,000. Winners sometimes got to meet prominent farmers or ranchers, such as when the young girl who raised the blue-ribbon Holstein calf at a New York State Fair got to show off her animal to the owner

"The fruit and vegetable display will be enormous," this broadside for the 1892 Minnesota State Fair promised.

of the world's largest cattle ranch. In 1954, President Dwight Eisenhower was on hand to present an award to a 4-H champion during Children's Day at the Eastern States Exposition in Massachusetts. "I believe your presence at such an exposition as this, competing in all the agricultural products of this great Northeast, is very fine," he said, "an essential step in becoming the good citizen you must be if America is to remain as our fathers handed it to us."

Exhibitions of farmyard bounty at fairs were not limited to livestock. Fruit, vegetables, and other crops were a large part of fairs from the very beginning. Describing his visit to a fair in 1853, Minnesota farmer Mitchell Jackson wrote: "There is a very respectable display of . . . Wheat Corn Potatoes & Fruit Particularly of Apples of which there is a good variety of the finest I ever saw Some weighing as high as 20 ounces (it is said). Agriculture is beginning to receive the attention which it deserves."

Jumbo apples implied fertile soil and good weather, which in turn meant that visitors might consider settling, thereby fulfilling another purpose of fairs. Growth was the order of the day. Early Minnesota fairs were partly aimed at convincing skeptical farmers that they could successfully raise corn and wheat in that state. In 1856, the Utah State Fair displayed large squashes, beets, carrots, wheat, corn, eggplants, grapes, peaches, and apples, dramatizing the range of crops suitable to the region.

Exhibits of crops and produce from individual counties rapidly became a standard (and highly competitive) feature of state fairs. Typical booths included three or four samples of every kind of fruit and vegetable grown in a county, painstakingly stacked and woven into intricate displays that were works of art themselves. Tall grasses would be gathered in June, then dried in a dark room so they'd keep their fragrance

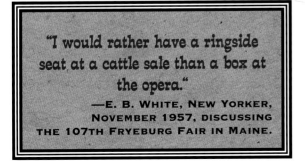

"I would rather have a ringside seat at a cattle sale than a box at the opera."
—E. B. WHITE, NEW YORKER, NOVEMBER 1957, DISCUSSING THE 107TH FRYEBURG FAIR IN MAINE.

WE WANT EVERYBODY . . . . .

TO ATTEND THE

# MINNESOTA STATE FAIR

AND

## EXPOSITION OF AGRICULTURE,

HAMLINE, MINN.,

## September 5, 6, 7, 8, 9, 10, '92

# $12,000 IN PREMIUMS

FOR

## Live Stock and Agricultural and Horticultural Exhibits

| | |
|---|---|
| The premium list has been revised, and competition in all classes is invited. | The fruit and vegetable display will be enormous. |
| The stock show, including horses, cattle, sheep and hogs, will surpass any previous year. | The ladies' department will contain every useful and ornamental household article. |
| The dairy department will be filled with the largest collection of dairy products in the United States. The manufacture of cheese will be one of the features of this division. | The popular FARMER'S INSTITUTE will be continued, with additional interesting features. |
| The poultry exhibit will include all the noted strains, home and foreign. | Friday will be "Farmer's Day." Mr. Jeremiah Simpson, of Kansas, is expected to be present, and will talk on topics of the day. |
| **ATTRACTIONS**<br>Are so arranged as to offer specialties each day. | **EXCITING RACES**<br>Each day of the Fair on one of the best tracks in the United States. |

## Visitors will find Instruction, Recreation and Enjoyment.

AMPLE ARRANGEMENTS FOR REFRESHMENTS ON THE GROUND.

Send for Premium List and Entry Blanks. The usual Reduced Rates on all Railroads. The Electric Street Cars run to the grounds from both Cities.

**Fairgoers visit a fruit wagon at the Pie Town, New Mexico, fair in 1940. No fruit was grown in that section of the country, which made fresh apples a real treat.**
Russell Lee/Library of Congress, LC-USF35-

when they were later twisted into the elaborate sheaves that decorated some exhibits.

Fairs often devised special contests for various fruits and vegetables, thereby producing some arresting displays. Exhibited at the Indiana fair in 1852 was an ear of corn with 30 rows of kernels (more than 1,800 in all) that shelled out to 1.3 quarts. In 1927 a farm journalist pointed out that "Indiana corn has been so standardized today that such an ear cannot be reproduced." Tall corn stalks, which had to bear at least one normal ear of corn, became a popular event at fairs in the Midwest. In 1938 two boys from Ollie, Iowa, won one such contest with a stalk nearly 16 feet tall. Three years later, a national con-

test at a fair was won with a 23-foot, 2.5-inch cornstalk. Farmers also vied to produce the longest string bean (a 37-incher won a prize at the Minnesota State Fair in 1921), or the largest sunflower. The Alaska State Fair introduced its well-known "Giant Cabbage" contest in 1941, when the manager of the Alaska Railroad donated a $25 prize to the person who grew a 23-pounder. Another sort of contest involved adults trying to guess how many pies might be made from a giant pumpkin, or the weight of the prizewinning hog (or, alternatively, how many pork chops that hog might produce).

Some contests required more participation than simply displaying animals or produce. Since the colonial era,

Stong) has been making butter sculptures since 1960. Such sculptures have been a fixture at the fair since the 1920s; her predecessor did the job for 36 years.

Lyons' biggest cow required 880 pounds of butter. She now starts with a wood and wire frame, so the finished product is not solid. Working in a glass-fronted booth kept between 38 degrees and 42 degrees, it takes her 16 hours to sculpt a cow. Lyons has sculpted all six breeds of dairy cows, horses, chickens, pigs, Elvis, Garth Brooks, and a replica of native son Grant Wood's "American Gothic." Lyons may well be the only artist in America whose training includes both sculpture and cow anatomy.

**As one of the largest industries in Florida, citrus deserves this special display at the 1964 Florida State Fair.**
Florida State Fair

**F. H. Beach (left), judge of fruits at the 1932 Indiana State Fair, and H. H. Swaim of South Bend, exhibitor and judge at the fair for the previous 40 years, confer before placing the sweepstakes ribbon. Beach was from Ohio State University.**

fairs featured several types of "work-play," which built cooperation between neighbors and enlivened the drudgery of daily labor. Logrollings and husking bees were quite popular. Corn-husking matches were held at exhibitions; contestants got shocks of corn with the same number of ears, and the winner was the man who shucked all of the ears clean and tied up the fodder the fastest. At the Chester County (Pennsylvania) fair in 1858, a farmer named Abraham Jackson husked 108 ears in 8 minutes. When York County held a countrywide contest in 1935, 65 contestants and 1,500 spectators attended. The 20 finalists husked for 80 minutes; the winner did 22 bushels of 70 pounds each. Local winners in turn went to a statewide contest, where, in front of 7,000 spectators, the champion in 1940 did 30 bushels.

Perhaps the most unusual attraction celebrating agricultural bounty is the butter sculpture. Begun to publicize the dairy industry, butter sculptures took hold at Midwestern fairs, as artists created huge likenesses of people and animals. At the 1903 Ohio State Fair, a butter company presented the fair's first butter cow and calf. The Illinois State Fair's Dairy Building, built in 1903, is now described as "home of the traditional butter cow for sixty years." At the 1950 Michigan State Fair, a butter sculpture of a cow and farmer, done by J. E. Wallace, required 450 pounds of butter.

Two particular butter-sculpting events have become noteworthy. At the Iowa State Fair, a cherubic woman named Norma "Duffy" Lyons (niece of author Phil

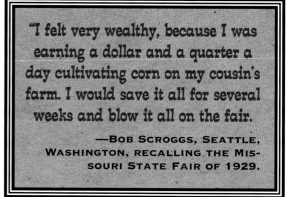

called the Glass Gazebo, wearing a ski jacket in order to keep warm. The butter busts then go on display. After the fair, princesses can take their heads home or donate them to a series of pancake breakfasts. The current butter sculptor, Linda Christensen, started in 1971, with a lifetime tally nearing 300 princesses.

In any state, eyeing the popular and highly impressive yellow creations, there is sure to be a young wisecracker in the crowd who'll cry, "Anybody got a piece of bread?"

State fairs offered a full spectrum of flora and fauna. The vegetable displays were serene and colorful: yellow corn, orange carrots, green beans, purple eggplant, each picture perfect and deserving both a ribbon and a spot on a plate at Sunday dinner. The livestock pavilions, in

**Citizens from Carbon County, Montana, erected this exhibit for the 1905 Montana State Fair to promote their land and achievements.**
Montana Historical Society, Helena

Dean Wright, sociology professor at Drake University, once described the importance of Lyons' work to Don Terry of the *New York Times* in 1996: "In London, people go to see the Queen's jewels. In Iowa, the butter cow is the star."

Lyons prefers to work with unsalted butter, and makes her sculptures at other fairs, too. She once did one in Maryland out of margarine, but she called it a "lousy" substitute when she had finished.

Another famous annual event features the winners of the Minnesota State Fair's "Princess Kay of the Milky Way" contest. Begun in 1953, the contest involves a statewide search for beauties, who get sculpted in butter while the public watches. The princesses take turns sitting in a glass-sided cooler

**Los Angeles County erected a stunning display for the 1932 California State Fair. Early county exhibits, dating back to the 1920s, focused on agriculture. Later, they included other types of industry, community topics, and tourism as themes.**
California State Fair

Horse-pulling contests remained popular in the Northeast and Midwest long after farmers stopped using draft horses for serious work. Horses pulled huge stone blocks in quarry country; more often, as in this photo, they worked against a mechanical device mounted in a truck. The chains on the truck's rear wheels kept powerful teams from pulling the whole contraption away. J. C. Allen and Son, Inc.

"The human animal is a gregarious creature, he (and she also) cannot thrive and be entirely happy if too lonesome. Therefore, when fair-time comes, he and all his family welcome the chance to get out, meet people, talk over crops, tatting, stock, canning, farm methods, cooking, see the sights, laugh—in a word to have a big holiday. And they go home when the fair is over, rejuvenated, refreshed, full of new ideas on stock, cooking, plowing, and how best to spank the unruly youngsters. The practical education of all has had a big boost, and the best part is, that it all seemed like playtime."
—THE SECRETARY OF THE FLUVANNA FAIR, IN THE MIDLAND VIRGINIAN, SEPTEMBER 1925.

**Today, some people raise draft horses as a hobby, trucking their Percherons, Shires, Belgians, and Clydesdales coast to coast to show them at fairs. This photo was taken in 1964.**
Iowa State Fair, Des Moines

Contestants line up for the tallest-corn-stalk contest at the 1938 Iowa State Fair. Any contest involving an "-est," whether it was biggest, fattest, smallest, oldest, or whatever, was a sure-fire crowd-pleaser at fairs. Iowa State Fair, Des Moines

contrast, were cacophonous. Sheep bleated constantly, roosters seemed to contest with their counterparts to see who was loudest. Everywhere owners scurried about, brushing, washing, and clipping their animals, eyeing the competition, trying hard to appear calm.

Things didn't quiet down until the fair ended. Once the scene of so much activity and anxiety, so much competition and concentration, so much triumph and disappointment, the pens and show rings began to empty. Describing his corner of the fair, farmer Cecil Barger wrote: "That night the hog pavilion became very quiet. The tenseness of the atmosphere was gone. The hogs grunted peacefully as they slept. Strings of ribbons, fluttering in the breeze, decorated each breeder's pens. Here and there under the lights were gathered little groups of men smoking cigars."

Memories mixed with plans. Next year, they thought, cogitating on recipes for pig food . . . next year. . . .

"In London, people go to see the Queen's jewels. In Iowa, the butter cow is the star."
—DEAN WRIGHT, SOCIOLOGY PROFESSOR AT DRAKE UNIVERSITY, DESCRIBING THE IMPORTANCE OF NORMA "DUFFY" LYONS' WORK TO DON TERRY OF THE NEW YORK TIMES.

Every year, a county beauty queen from Minnesota is chosen to reign as Princess Kay of the Milky Way at the state fair, and (as part of the honor) gets sculpted in butter. In 1956 Ruth Marie Peterson of Lansing was thus immortalized. Minnesota State Fair

# CHAPTER THREE

# Watching a Tractor Go Round in a Circle

Although seasonal fairs were already traditional during the early 19th century, they grew in popularity because of their focus on the future, not their roots in the past. For farmers (and, eventually, their families), an annual visit to the state fair was a chance to see improvements and innovations.

Because state governments saw fairs as a public opportunity to appear progressive and prosperous, fairs put a high priority on impressing visitors. The program for New Jersey's Great Inter-State Fair in 1893 proudly mentioned that the fair organizers had installed a mile of 2-inch iron water pipe and fittings for the convenience of fair exhibitors and visitors, an investment that paid off when the original water supply gave out. Other fairs installed electric lights (the Ohio State Fair claims that, in 1896, it was the first fair to do so).

Electric street cars carried people to the Indiana fairground in 1897; one of the attractions of the new conveyance was "no dust!" Beginning in 1899, the St. Paul Gaslight Company began extending mains throughout the Minnesota fairground to provide gas for light and heat. Bright lights meant fairs could offer entertainment after dark. The Ohio fair held races, concerts, and exhibitions. When Minnesota brought electricity to its fairground in 1901, it drew 19,000 people to nighttime shows.

Although rural folk earned reputations for being conventional and conservative, they relished novelties. Each passing decade brought a new vision of what things would be like in the unpredictable days ahead. The adjective "modern" remained a potent lure; at the Minnesota State Fair in 1920, customers at a 50¢, all-you-can-eat buffet selected their plates from a conveyor belt, an experience touted as the future of dining. When the South Dakota fair added a children's playground in 1926, the fair advertised "modern devices to amuse children."

The importance of inventions far exceeded their application to entrees and teeter-totters, of course. Farmers battled crushing workloads and welcomed labor-saving devices, but had few ways to find out about them. Before radio and television began delivering an onslaught of advertising, state fairs were a prime means of introducing new tools and methods to large, dispersed rural audiences.

Most school children, taking exams after their lessons on early-19th-century agriculture, could readily identify Cyrus McCormick as the inventor of an extremely successful reaping machine. They may not have learned how a fair provided a key step in his career. McCormick's father, a blacksmith, had futilely worked on the device for 20 years before turning it over to Cyrus, his eldest son. Cyrus gradually perfected the machine, demonstrated it in public for the first time in 1831, and patented it three years later. Yet for a decade his customers were local farmers. The first

> "He would set one of his tractors going in a circle. And it would just go all the time, all day long. People would come and look at it, and watch."
>
> —JOURNALIST RICHARD JACKSON OF GREENCASTLE, INDIANA, DESCRIBING A FAMILY FRIEND WHO HAD BEEN THE STATE DISTRIBUTOR FOR MOLINE PLOWS AND TRACTORS.

**Two young men examine the newest offering from John Deere at a county fair in Ohio in 1938.** Ben Shahn/Library of Congress, LC-USF33-6651-M1

well-designed machines had cut that time to just 10 minutes. A hard-working man could cut an acre a day with a scythe; a mechanical reaper or mower could slice through 15 acres in the same amount of time. Breakthroughs like these show why exhibitions of improved tools and labor-saving inventions became the centerpiece of fairs in the middle and late 1800s.

Old and young, rich and poor, people crowded around displays and exhibitions, asking questions, offering opinions, and carefully weighing the pros and cons of potential purchases. Author Willard Lange summarized a typical gathering of farmers at a fair in Georgia in the middle of the 19th century: "Tales were being

Many a fairgoer saw his or her first moving pictures at a state fair. This antique apparatus is among the thousands of artifacts housed at the Minnesota State Fair museum. Minnesota State Fair

formal recognition of the value of his invention came with a certificate of merit at a fair in Hamilton County, Ohio, in 1844. Word spread rapidly after that. Demand was such that, within three years, McCormick's manufacturing plant in Chicago was the largest factory west of Pittsburgh.

Farmers wanted to find ways to make their work easier and faster, and within their lifetimes, they saw astonishing improvements. In 1830 a farmer spent more than three hours harvesting a bushel of wheat. By 1880

This giant electric numeral went up on the Minnesota State Fair grandstand in 1909, just after electricity began adding even more hours of fun to the classic day at the fair. No longer did folks have to head home at dusk.
Minnesota State Fair

swapped of the success or failure of newfangled inventions," such as mechanical cotton planters, corn huskers and shellers, riding cultivators, hay loaders, and presses. Only at fairs could farmers actually watch new devices at work and gauge their performance.

In the early years of American agricultural fairs, farmers were intensely interested in new plows. Although a display of a silver-plated plow drew laughter from farmers at the first Iowa State Fair in 1854, plows were the primal tool of farming, something that every planter and homesteader needed, regardless of their crops. Plows appear on the state seals of Pennsylvania, Tennessee, and New Jersey, testimony to the tool's historic prominence. Yet any farmer with an ounce of imagination could see that plows were inefficient tools. Existing designs were awkward and clumsy; the results were often mediocre. In the 1830s, farmers sometimes needed huge teams to pull bulky plowshares that weighed up to 125 pounds over hard, hilly soil. In more forgiving dirt, a farmer might make do with a pair of horses or oxen; even so, he was glad to finish an acre and a half a day.

An old-style plow, made of cast iron, was acceptable for the soils of the East, but not for those of the Midwest, where the deep roots of prairie plants slowed it down and

Folks attended fairs to see inventions and innovations, to sample the modern along with the traditional as "newfangled" and "old-fashioned" continued their perpetual *pas de deux*. Horses may have stopped pulling plows and serving as the primary source of transportation, but they kept performing in shows and rodeos at fairs.
Ohio Expositions Commission and
C. LaVon Shook

In 1830 a farmer spent more than three hours harvesting a bushel of wheat. By 1880 well-designed machines had cut that time to just ten minutes.

1852 • 1952

CENTENNIAL ANNIVERSARY

INDIANA STATE FAIR

AUGUST 28 • SEPT. 6

**What better way to symbolize a century of farming progress than an old, single-bottom, horse-drawn plow and a modern, multiple-bottom, tractor-drawn version?**
Indiana State Fair

dirt collected on the plow's surface. Farmers had to stop and clean the blade every 100 feet or less. The United States Patent Office issued more than 100 patents for "prairie plows" before 1830, and all were failures.

Specialized plows were the order of the day at state fairs between 1850 and 1880. Inventors designed plows for clay, light sandy soil, alluvial or muck soil, and subsoil. Paring plows cut roots without leaving furrows; the reversed moldboards on hillside plows threw dirt on the downhill side. At the Indiana State Fair of 1876, fairgoers could scrutinize 35 different breaking plows. Awarding ribbons, prizes, and premiums, judges evaluated new designs for how much the plow weighed, how much power it required to cut and turn a furrow, the depth of the furrows it cut, what it was made from, its workmanship, durability, and price.

Farmers debated the pros and cons of the sulky plow, which had been introduced in the mid-1860s. One fair superintendent declared them ineligible for premiums, believing them to be impractical. A proponent, however, argued that riding plows would be ideal for women, and for men who were weak or crippled. New designs were already reducing the draft of plows, which in turn increased the acreage that a farmer could plow in a day. Because extra power was available, the farmer could ride without undue strain on the animals, or he could add another bottom to

his plow and get twice as much done. By the 1880s, the controversy had ended: sulky plows were commonplace from Ohio to Iowa.

The tools used for other repetitive, back-breaking jobs were also ripe for replacement. One had long been gathering dust in museums and antique stores when, in 1959, the manager of the Oregon State Fair got an

> "Typically, a fiddler, chorus, and a dance caller would provide the cues and music from a small stage, while a quartet of the new tractors, each one pulling a two-bottom plow, a disk harrow, a cargo platform, or a corn planter, went through their paces.... They even got the tractors to bow at the end."

manual labor that they sold themselves. Reapers were complex enough to offer lots of room for minor improvements. Nine combined reaper-mowers "hotly contested" a $100 gold medal at the Indiana State Fair in 1876, one account said. Eight single reapers and single mowers competed for $50 gold medals, as well. By the 1920s, combines had advanced so dramatically that two men could do the work of twenty.

Farmers had to choose between oxen, cattle, horses, and mules to pull their implements. Steam engines of varying sizes were harnessed to some implements, with mixed results. With the addition of wheels, the stage was set for the arrival of the most revolutionary invention

These John Deere tractors at the 1930 Indiana State Fair show that the age of the pneumatic tire was still in the future (it was introduced two years later). J. C. Allen and Son, Inc.

unusual letter from a woman in Idaho. She offered a season ticket from the 1867 fair in exchange for tickets to the current fair. The fair manager leaped at the chance to acquire such a rare item. The ticket was decorated with a steel engraving of a young farmer sharpening a scythe, a tool associated with what one historian called the "era of the flail and the sickle" before the Civil War. When the Oregon ticket was printed, reaping and mowing machines were already on the market. The Illinois State Fair in 1857 included both. At fairs during the next 20 years, as many as two dozen different types of reapers and mowers would be on display.

Fair organizers were always alert for ways to show off new implements. At a state fair in 1860, inventor John Manny demonstrated his combined reaper-mower by cutting the grass and hazel brush on the race track infield. Some machines were so obviously superior to

"Tales were being swapped of the success or failure of newfangled inventions."
—AUTHOR WILLARD LANGE, SUMMARIZING A TYPICAL GATHERING OF FARMERS AT A FAIR IN GEORGIA IN THE MIDDLE OF THE 19TH CENTURY.

Aficionados of old equipment will find much to enjoy in this scene from the Iowa State Fair's version of machinery hill. The ramps at center left were built to display the climbing power of the unusual tracked tractor parked on the overpass. State Historical Society of Iowa, Des Moines

Gulf Oil piggybacked on the tractor displays at this Indiana State Fair. The man in the white shirt at center is holding a small powered tiller. The Ford tractor exhibit was to the far right.
*Indiana State Fair*

ever to appear at fairs: the tractor. New mechanical implements did more work but demanded more power. A corn picker, invented before the Civil War, vastly increased production to about eight acres per day, more than four times what a man using a knife could do. Unfortunately, it took too much power to pull the new machine. In the late 1850s, demonstrations of huge steam tractors had excited crowds and attracted lots of publicity when their manufacturers demonstrated them on hard ground. The inflated expectations of spectators and tractormakers alike, however, quickly deflated when the gigantic machines bogged down on damp soils.

A few steam tractors were in use in wheat country by the turn of the century, drawing threshing machines, but elsewhere, horses and mules were still standard, and most small farmers could afford only one or two working animals.

The real spur to the development of an efficient and practical tractor was World War I, which immediately drained manpower across the farm belt. At fairs, tractors were touted as the ideal replacement for farm hands who had gone off to fight in Europe.

As with plows a couple generations earlier, interest in the machines was intense. Regular improvements were showcased at fairs, such as the "power takeoff" (which allowed farmers to use the tractor engine to power an implement by means of a shaft), introduced in

Men, women, and children alike gathered to watch this tractor, powered by a Case engine, crawl up an artificial hill in 1907. Because this card was sent to Emma Manry of Goggansville, Georgia, the fair mentioned on the front was probably the Georgia State Fair.

Souvenir of the Fair—Case Engine Doing Stunts.

*How are you? We went out to the fair one day and had a fine time. Let us hear from you sometimes. Aff. Isabel R.*

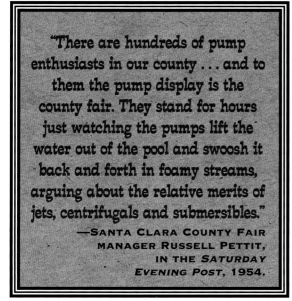

1918, or pneumatic tires (which made tractors faster, more comfortable, and more fuel-efficient, and which lasted longer than the older designs) in 1932. Most farmers recall the old steel wheels with little enthusiasm; "They shook you terrible," one remarked.

Tractormakers had sold just 600 machines in 1907; by 1950, farmers owned 3,400,000 of them. A tractor was parked in a barn or shed on virtually every farm in every county in America. Only Amish farmers and others devoted to simpler ways of life did without.

Barring major advances in the design or capability of their machines, tractormakers relied on gimmicks to attract attention. In the 1950s, International Harvester staged a series of tractor square dances at state fairs. Typically, a fiddler, chorus, and a dance caller provided the cues and music from a small stage, while a quartet of the new tractors, each one pulling a two-bottom plow, a disk harrow, a cargo platform, or a corn planter, went through their paces. "It was something to watch," recalls Sunny Sinnamon, a longtime official at the Indiana State Fair. "They even got the tractors to bow at the end."

To sell tractors, manufacturers touted horsepower or fuel economy when they didn't have something substantial. The introduction of the continuous power take-off in the early 1950s attracted much attention: before, when the tractor was taken out of gear, the drive belt stopped, interrupting the work. Belts had been dangerous, as well; "They would flop around and come off," one farmer recalls. "A lot of guys got killed by them."

Another breakthrough at that time involved hydraulics, which made the raising and lowering of

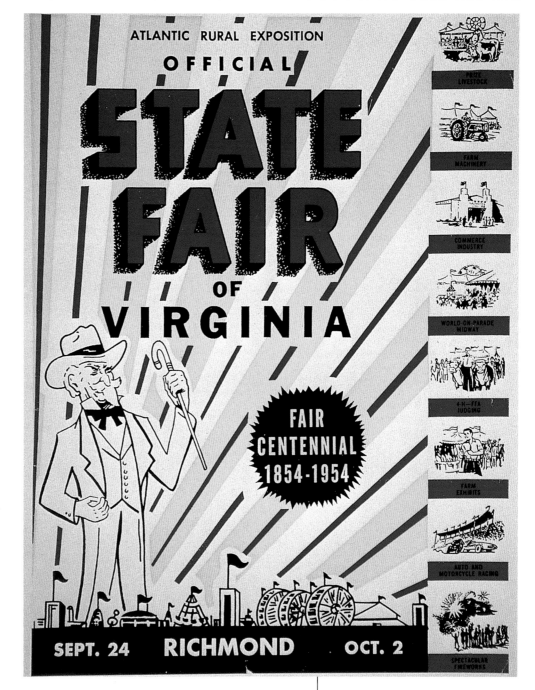

various tractor-driven implements much easier. Various other improvements appeared, sometimes coaxing farmers to spring for a new machine. The starter on early tractors was a heavy metal wheel on the side of the engine that the farmer had to spin by hand; this device was eventually replaced. Early tractors had seats attached to a curved piece of steel, like that on a leaf spring; when a seat with a shock absorber and a large

The fair's exhibits of farm machinery (symbolized by the tractor, second from the top at right) held the potent promise of farm work done faster, cheaper, easier, or better—four things sure to interest any farmer. State Fair of Virginia

**Tractors routinely last for decades on farms, so it generally took something exceptional to make a farmer part with a reliable old machine that was paid for and that ran fine. Here, members of a Future Farmers of America club see if this Ford Workmaster has what it takes at the 1959 Florida State Fair.**
Florida State Fair

fect solution. Unfortunately, just two years after the machines appeared, they were made obsolete when farmers discovered that dynamite was cheaper and easier (and probably more fun, as well).

Small utility engines, on the other hand, were a solid success. The Indiana State Fair displayed some one-horsepower models as early as 1876. They ran on natural gas, at an estimated cost of 25¢ for five hours. By the first decade of the 20th century, single-cylinder gasoline engines were standard gear for small farms, where they powered sawmills, ran feed-grinders, and pumped water. Some had wheels, others were stationary. Equipped with a flat pulley, they could run a washing machine; with a five-horsepower engine, a farmer could cut wood. Often, the town blacksmith was also the town mechanic; in the 1920s, he used to charge $2 to get the engines running. The small engines were sturdy and reliable. Some ran oil wells all day for 15 years without needing major repairs.

spring appeared, farmers eyed the invention with appreciation.

Early enclosed tractors, such as the Ford 8N or 9N, had canvas enclosures; the cab drew heat from the engine in winter, but the enclosures were stifling.

Sinnamon vividly remembers the introduction of the John Deere 4010 in the early 1960s, because it was such a dramatic improvement, with its six-cylinder engine, power brakes, power steering, and comfortable seat. It was introduced in Indiana at the state fair, and Sinnamon and other farmers made a point of checking it out.

Some inventions succeeded, others failed. Clearing forested land, farmers found it easy to chop down trees but hard to uproot the stumps. Thus, in the early 1870s, mechanical stump pullers seemed like the per-

The rural electric co-ops in the early 1930s knocked these small gas engines right out of existence, for the most part. As is the case with so many old tools, these old "one-lunger" engines are now popular features at state fair antique tool shows. At a recent Iowa State Fair, a gas-engine club livened up their exhibit by running an assortment of antique machines. The oldest was built in 1898 (it used a type of fuel called distillate). Nearby was a 1915 1.5-horsepower engine that originally cost $65, and a 1919 Rock Island 2-horsepower model running a little corn grinder. The repetitive pops of the old engines were unerringly distinctive.

Companies continually sought creative ways to draw customers to their displays. At Michigan state fairs

"I remember seeing the big John Deere two-cylinder D running along while setting on four Coke bottles. See, it does run smoothly, even on two cylinders! The Caterpillar exhibit had a four-cylinder injector pump set up with an electric motor drive. The injectors would squirt their fuel over a burning wick and made a nice shot of flame as each one 'fired.'"

—CHARLES KIZER, HARRISBURG, OREGON, RECALLING THE OREGON STATE FAIR OF THE MID-1930S.

Small, durable and versatile gas engines quickly became essential on small farms across the country. This nicely restored version was putt-putting away at the 1998 Iowa State Fair, thanks to a local club of collectors. The brand name makes it clear how the manufacturer touted this product.

in the early 1930s, for example, the Ford Motor Company let fairgoers test-drive new cars on a special half-mile track. At the 1941 Indiana State Fair, purely to attract attention, the manager of a local tractor company put a diesel tractor in a huge, glass-walled tank of water, cranked it up, and used it to power a treadmill. To the delight of hot and thirsty fairgoers, a maker of milk coolers once handed out cups of cool drinking water from one of his machines.

Although early fairs awarded cash prizes, trophies, and ribbons to the manufacturers of new pieces of equipment, mechanical exhibits soon became opportunities to show and sell rather than compete. Sometimes judges noted their approval in their official reports to the state board of agriculture, a mention that proved useful in advertisements.

The shows grew bigger and more popular. By the 1920s, large Midwestern fairs typically had up to 80 acres of farm machinery. And by the late 1940s, half of all national manufacturers participated in at least one large fair. In 1953, the Texas State Fair had 252,000 square feet of exhibit space.

Farm equipment remained the largest category, but fairgoers also saw demonstrations of washing machines, heaters, and ventilating equipment. An "electric farm exhibit" at the 1953 Minnesota fair included chick brooding equipment, pumps, milk handling tanks, ventilating equipment, and silage defrosters, all powered by electricity.

Displays often had a local bent. In breezy places, windmills spun their vanes; at the 1954 Florida State Fair, attic exhaust fans, cellar dehumidifiers, and prefab houses drew large crowds. Out West, irrigation equipment was important. Describing the Santa Clara County Fair to a writer from the *Saturday Evening Post* in 1954, manager Russell Pettit observed: "There are hundreds of pump enthusiasts in our county . . . and to

them the pump display is the county fair. They stand for hours just watching the pumps lift the water out of the pool and swoosh it back and forth in foamy streams, arguing about the relative merits of jets, centrifugals and submersibles."

Sunny Sinnamon, who attended fairs in the late 1940s and early 1950s with his grandparents, remembers liking the machinery exhibits the best. "You hated livestock," he jokes. "They stunk, and you had to work around them."

Whether a farmer was looking for a major implement or a specialized device, Machinery Hill was the place to go. A farmer might need a hog trap, or a tool for chopping the heads off chickens. The Ohio State Fair started a Farm Gadget contest in the late 1940s, giving awards for labor-saving devices. Who knew someone would bring in the equivalent of the gimlet posthole digger? A simple enough idea, but every farmer who had ever dug postholes with a shovel—which was just about every farmer whoever raised livestock—agreed it deserved a blue ribbon, if not a gold medal.

49

# CHAPTER FOUR

# The Most Reckless, Fearless Men and Women Who've Ever Lived

Even the most honest people enjoy watching death get cheated. Daredevils turned this public interest into a moneymaker: the fair thrill show. Since the earliest state fairs, brave and innovative riders, pilots, acrobats, drivers, and divers have risked their lives to entertain large audiences. The greater the danger, the bigger the crowd. Fearless men and women delighted fairgoers with hair-raising stunts from vehicles and platforms, wires and poles—flying, hanging, jumping and diving, and sometimes crashing. Most of the time death lost out. Sometimes, it didn't.

## BALLOONS, DIRIGIBLES, AND PLANES

Advertisements for the 1952 Nebraska State Fair heralded an unusual stunt: an old-fashioned balloon ascension, "such as very few young folks have ever seen," the ads said. During his show, the balloonist climbed to 4,000 feet, then leaped out and floated to earth in a parachute. The colorful balloon against the blue summer sky and the tiny figure plummeting earthward made for a crowd-pleasing stunt. The youngsters in the audience probably didn't realize that their ancestors had watched similar performances a century earlier.

This 1952 show was a nostalgic glance back at the generations of daredevils who made a living by risking death (or at least appearing to), and who helped make the state fair thrill show into a central attraction. Balloon ascensions got top billing in the years after the Civil War. Balloonists gave way to wing-walkers and stunt pilots in the air, and to lead-footed, foolhardy drivers on the ground.

> "The thrill that brings you closest to death is the one that pleases the mob most. Some of them even resent it if you're not actually killed."
>
> —"IT'S EASY IF YOU HAVE THE NERVE," SIG SMITH, *COLLIER'S*, MARCH 1936

Acrobats teetered on high wires and did headstands on tall, swaying poles; divers leaped from 100 feet into tanks of water topped with blazing gasoline. Anything that involved noisy collisions and explosions was a sure-fire hit.

Today, mildly adventurous tourists hop in hot-air balloons and float over the countryside, sipping champagne. In the beginning, though, ballooning was the domain of risk-takers. At state fairs between the Civil War and the turn of the century, balloons drew huge crowds because they were unusual and unreliable.

The early shows didn't always go as planned. During the Minnesota State Fair's first balloon ascension (in 1863), a strong wind came up and carried the balloon away so quickly that the crowd barely got a chance to see it. But the shows were enjoyable enough that they gradually developed a huge following. Audiences of 20,000 watched famous balloonists such as John Wise of Lancaster, Pennsylvania. He billed himself as "the world-renowned aeronaut who has made more voyages through the heavens than any other man." His fame derived from a series of record-setting flights, including an 1858 voyage from St. Louis to Henderson, New York, that took 20 hours and covered 1,120 miles. This distance record stood for 41 years; the fact that Wise had

**Whether these kids were watching a high-wire act or a wing-walker on a biplane, their expressions make it clear why thrill day at a state fair was an event not to be missed. This photo was taken in 1936.** Iowa State Fair, Des Moines

Balloon ascensions eventually became old hat to fairgoing crowds, and not even the innovation of female balloonists could keep them alive as an attraction. During their heyday, however, balloon flights were high drama, indeed.
Minnesota State Fair

meant to cross the Atlantic didn't matter to the public.

Another air voyage, 1,000 miles shorter, grabbed headlines during the Illinois State Fair in 1858, which featured exhibitions by balloonist Samuel Wilson. One afternoon he tethered his balloon to a fence on a farm owned by a man named Benjamin Harvey, next to the fairgrounds. Curious folks climbed in and out of the basket, examining the apparatus and perhaps pretending that they, too, were brave enough to trust their lives to hot air, wicker, and hemp. The rope holding the balloon broke just after Harvey's two youngest children (aged eight and three) had climbed into the basket. Horrified bystanders watched helplessly as the huge balloon lurched into the air and wobbled off.

Wilson leaped on one of Mr. Harvey's horses and galloped to town to spread the alarm. Frantic messages fanned out via telegraph and railroad, asking people to watch for the runaway balloon. Family and friends spent an anxious night. The balloon was finally located the next morning on a farm 18 miles away. The two children were unharmed; newspapers reported that the youngest was asleep.

Every near-miss and outright disaster added to the allure of the dubious contraptions, but audiences were uncomfortable admitting it. Purely commercial entertainment still wasn't respectable; hard-working, God-fearing folk weren't supposed to have a bloodthirsty streak. Some balloonists called themselves "professor" to lend their flights an aura of scientific research. At the Indiana State Fair in 1869, for example, a Professor Wilbur made two ascensions, earning $100 per flight.

Inevitably, however, simple ascensions became routine. Even the mainly uneducated and sheltered crowds at state fairs proved to be fickle and easily bored. By 1892 one of the organizers of the Indiana State Fair went on record as saying that audiences were no longer attracted to the sight of a balloon rising 3,000 feet in the air. In the late 1880s, at state fairs in Rhode Island and Pennsylvania, young couples had already gotten married in balloons and sailed off in them, honeymoon-bound. To give the spectators some-

thing dramatic, balloonists began leaping out of their baskets wearing parachutes.

French balloonist Jacques Garnerin had done this stunt nearly a century earlier with sensational results, ascending several thousand feet, cutting loose his basket, then contriving to explode his balloon as he parachuted free. According to author Fulgence Marion in *Wonderful Balloon Ascents*, the balloon's explosion "forced a sudden

"Men refused to believe their eyes and children stood in amazement."
—ACCOUNT OF DIRIGIBLE FLIGHT AT OHIO STATE FAIR, 1906.

A balloon ascends at the Montana state fairground in Helena in 1885. For a few years, just watching the ungainly devices float off was enough to satisfy customers in the grandstand. Later, the aeronauts had to be more creative.
Montana Historical Society, Helena

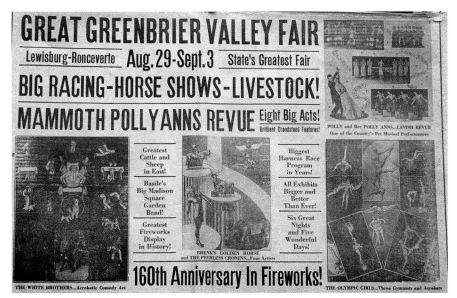

GREAT GREENBRIER VALLEY FAIR

Lewisburg-Ronceverte   Aug. 29-Sept. 3   State's Greatest Fair

BIG RACING-HORSE SHOWS-LIVESTOCK!

MAMMOTH POLLY ANNS REVUE   Eight Big Acts!
Brilliant Grandstand Features!

POLLY and Her POLLY ANNS...LAVISH REVUE
One of the Country's Pet Musical Performances

Greatest Cattle and Sheep in East!

Basile's Big Madison Square Garden Band!

Greatest Fireworks Display in History!

Biggest Harness Race Program in Years!

All Exhibits Bigger and Better Than Ever!

Six Great Nights and Five Wonderful Days!

BRENK'S GOLDEN HORSE and THE PEERLESS CRONINS...Four Artists

160th Anniversary In Fireworks!

THE WHITE BROTHERS...Acrobatic Comedy Act

THE OLYMPIC GIRLS...Three Gymnasts and Acrobats

**Newspaper ads piled on the superlatives—Biggest! Greatest! Newest!—when promoting an upcoming fair. This ad for the State Fair of West Virginia touts acrobats, gymnasts, a "lavish revue," and the "Greatest Fireworks Display in History." The latter claim was impossible to prove, of course, but why not find out for yourself?**
Eamswood Communications, Inc., for the State Fair of West Virginia

cry of fear from the whole multitude, and made a number of women faint."

American balloonists began duplicating Garnerin's feat at the turn of the century, sometimes hidden in torpedo-like objects that were suspended in place of the usual basket. At a height of several thousand feet, it exploded to release the parachutist.

Stunts such as this one were obviously hazardous, and the body count climbed. A young balloonist named Harry Davis died in an accident in Delphos, Ohio, on August 22, 1900. He had parachuted from his balloon at 800 feet, only to find that his ropes were entangled. To the horror of spectators, Davis slammed into a telegraph wire before his body hit the ground. Doctors found that he had no broken bones and only a few scratches, but, as contemporary newspaper accounts pointed out with macabre detail, he had been "crushed internally to a pulp."

Technology, not mishaps, spelled the end of balloons as attractions. The future became apparent at the Indiana State Fair in 1906, when a dirigible was the center of attention. At the Ohio State Fair that year, one account said, "Men refused to believe their eyes and children stood in amazement" while an airship flew from the fairgrounds to the state capitol and back. Airship flights highlighted the Indiana fair and others the following year. The stage was set for the next generation of aeronautic exhibitions by vehicles that were faster, louder, stronger, and more dangerous: airplanes.

In an editorial in July 1909, *Billboard* accurately predicted "the aeroplane will be the great sensational attraction of the year at State Fairs." Iowa had already had an airship at its fair in 1906, when a lighter-than-air device flew two miles to the capitol and back again. The first airplane flight in Minnesota took place at the state fairgrounds in 1910. At the Illinois State Fair, the early biplanes— notably the Curtiss JN-4D "Jenny"—used the infield of the one-mile track as an airstrip, landing at speeds as slow as 35 miles per hour.

Barnstormers such as Walter Brookins, a member of the Wright brothers' flying team, drew huge audiences after newspapers reported such record-breaking feats as Brookins' 1910 speed record, a flight from Chicago to the Illinois fairgrounds in Springfield that took a mere seven hours (he had to land only twice to refuel).

At fairs across the country, folks packed the wooden grandstands to watch the likes of Lincoln Beachey, the

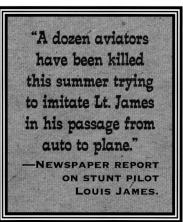

"A dozen aviators have been killed this summer trying to imitate Lt. James in his passage from auto to plane."
—NEWSPAPER REPORT ON STUNT PILOT LOUIS JAMES.

**Roy Knabenshue of Toledo, Ohio, brought his airship Toledo II to the 1906 Ohio State Fair. He had first appeared the previous year, and returned with various lighter-than-air craft each year through 1908. He walked back and forth on the cane-fiber walkway beneath the air bag to maneuver. Later versions held several passengers.**
Ohio Expositions Commission and C. LaVon Shook

prototypical barnstormer. Dressed in a suit and wearing a high, starched collar, Beachey swept past the crowd a foot off the ground, with his arms flung wide and steering with his knees. He retired in 1912 at age 25 because "he had come to believe the public only wanted to see him kill himself," wrote Paul O'Neil in *Barnstormers and Speed Kings*, "and . . . because newspapers had begun blaming him for the deaths of aviators who tried to imitate him."

To attract crowds, the 1911 Iowa State Fair issued promotions that announced, "Wright Brothers' Birdmen Are Coming." At daily exhibitions, fairgoers could see the famous machines that had set such distance records as a 106-mile nonstop flight in Texas the previous year, and an altitude record of 11,474 feet in Los Angeles.

The Indiana State Fair of 1914 featured both monoplanes (which were less common than the more familiar biplanes, and usually used for racing) and "Wright flying machines" (these were biplanes but not necessarily built by the Wrights themselves).

Beachey eventually returned to his hazardous trade and died in a crash on March 14, 1915, while doing a stunt in front of a crowd of 50,000 at the Panama-Pacific Exposition in San Francisco. Similar tragedies seemed only to fuel the public's demand for airborne thrills, spurring increasingly hazardous stunts. On the upper wing of biplanes, wing-walkers simulated tennis matches, did headstands, or sat on anchored chairs pretending to

**Pilot J. C. Marr makes his first flight in Montana at the Montana State Fair, September 26, 1910. The airplane's propeller became an exhibit at a local aviation museum.**
Montana Historical Society, Helena

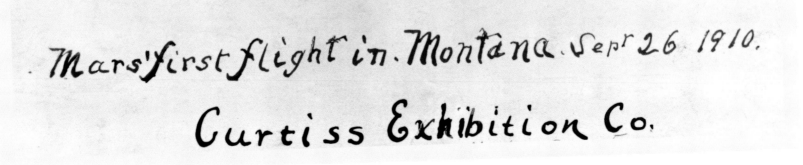

*Mars' first flight in Montana. Sept 26, 1910.*
*Curtiss Exhibition Co.*

Lillian Boyer wows 'em at the 1923 Minnesota State Fair, as women achieved gender equity in the hair-raising job of wing-walking. Minnesota State Fair

read newspapers. They rode the wings through barrel rolls, loops, and spins. Ormer Locklear earned notoriety by jumping or climbing from the wing of one aircraft to another, and once dropped from a plane into a train. Between August and November 1919, he performed at 22 air shows and fairs in 15 states. In grim echoes of Beachey's experience, eight imitators died while copying his stunts, and he survived numerous brushes with death. Once, during a midair transfer at the Illinois State Fair, he almost fell when the weighted bar at the bottom of the transfer ladder smacked him in the forehead, opening a bloody gash. Locklear died at age 29 in August 1920, doing a nighttime stunt for a motion picture.

By then, stunt flying was a popular and lucrative business, full of daredevils looking for a gimmick. At the Minnesota State Fair in 1917, Katherine Stinson, the first woman to loop an airplane, performed. Two years earlier, Ruth Law, one of the first female stunt flyers, had done a parachute jump and what ads called "fancy flying" at the Indiana State Fair. She was the first female aviator to appear at the fair. Female pilots were a novelty, and thus highly sought as attractions. The demand convinced Buffalo Bill Cody's niece Mabel to abandon her career as a circus acrobat and to take up stunt flying.

Law's brother, a film stunt man and parachutist, had inspired her to approach the famous Orville Wright for lessons; he refused, but offered to sell her a plane, which she bought and quickly learned to fly. By the late 1910s, Ruth Law's Flying Circus and its crew of 10 pilots was a familiar attraction at large fairs and air shows. For publicity purposes, Law sometimes took her police dog, Poilu, flying with her (she once told a reporter that a wounded French officer had given her the dog). While speaking to a civic group in Columbus, Ohio, in 1918, Law revealed that the government had canceled her permit to fly for the duration of the war.

At the Minnesota State Fair in 1921, one of her stars was 19-year-old Louis James, who awed the audiences by hanging from the landing gear of a plane by his toes or his teeth. Law had tried to dissuade the youth when he first applied for a job by telling him he would have to walk out on the wing his first time up. He did it effortlessly, explaining later that he'd learned his stunts in the rafters of his father's barn, showing off for his friends.

Interviewed by reporters at the Minnesota fair, Law told of her closest call: she was doing a loop at night with fireworks on the plane when a flash temporarily blinded her. She inadvertently flew over the chimney of a blast furnace, and her aircraft plummeted from a height of 1,500 feet to just 500 feet before she regained control.

Without question, stunt flying was an extremely risky business. Touting the fearlessness of Louis James,

"If [the engine fails], I have an arrangement with the pilot to sort of swipe me sideways along the grass rather than let the ship crash down on me."
—HELICOPTER STUNT MAN RAMON "BUDDY" LARUE.

Stunt pilot Captain Frank F. "Bowser" Frakes swoops toward his target at the 1935 Minnesota State Fair thrill show. His amazing career left a million memories with awe-struck fairgoers who watched him crash squadrons of antique aircraft into specially made houses.
Minnesota Historical Society

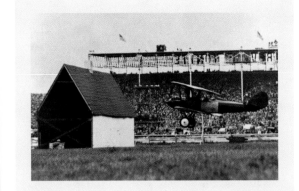

Frakes built the structures he crashed into so that they would collapse and help absorb the impact of the collisions. The aircraft were always destroyed, and the audiences were invariably impressed. Captain Frakes seemed to have made little impression on the formal historical record; however, when I found a reference to a July 1951 article in *Flying* magazine entitled "He Walked Away From 99 Crashes," I knew the article could only be about one person.

## Why Crowds Liked Balloon Ascensions

These airborne stunts were popular because fair managers were "hoping that an accident might happen by which a human being would fall from the skies and flatten out on the ground in the presence of thousands of applauding citizens, who would go home and say they never had such a good time at a fair. Many societies have felt hurt that the balloonist came down safely, and in some cases, where the balloonist has fallen to death a mile or two away from the fairground, the management has complained and held back the money from the heirs of the deceased, on the ground that the death exhibit was not what they had a right to expect. But the balloon part of an agricultural fair has become too free from casualties to be attractive, and new attractions are sought."

—*BILLBOARD*, AUGUST 9, 1899.

newspapers noted that "a dozen aviators have been killed this summer trying to imitate Lieutenant James in his passage from auto to plane."

By 1927, so many stunt pilots had killed themselves that the federal authorities prohibited aircraft from flying within 300 feet of each other, or from carrying fireworks or explosives. Pilots kept dreaming up new feats anyway. In the 1930s, a Canadian war ace named Dick Granere did tailspins at just 300 feet. He dropped down to hedge-hopping height to leapfrog parked cars. His signature performance featured two large wooden frames that held fabric targets about 40 feet in diameter. He flew through the first target, did a loop and a half roll, then sliced through the second one.

Even more spectacular were the amazing exploits of Capt. F. F. "Bowser" Frakes, a barnstormer and one-time flight instructor who quit a job as a test pilot to concentrate on thrill shows. Frakes and a couple of his cronies had been looking for a new gimmick after the stock market crash of 1929; crowds for simulated dogfights, low-level aerobatics, and wing-walking had dwindled. Together they thought of wrecking a plane on purpose; Frakes drew the short straw and tried it first, a relatively modest ground loop in 1931 that tore off one wing and broke the landing gear on a Stearman.

Frakes didn't invent this stunt; the 1925 price list from a flight team called the 13 Black Cats specified that a crash "into trees, houses, etc." cost $1,200; one of their pilots would crash head-on into an automobile for $250. Frakes, however, took this lunatic genre to new heights. Soon he was smashing into board walls, barns, mountains, and the bare ground. He tried crashing into a large pond at Lakewood Park in Atlanta in 1935, but decided it was too dangerous. His aircraft of choice was whatever old plane he could buy near where he was scheduled to perform: he crashed Swallows, Travelaires, Jennies, Wacos, DeHavillands, and Gypsy Moths.

Frakes also did auto stunts, including one in which he bounced across some railroad tracks just in front of a speeding train. He claimed to have invented the stunt of crashing an auto through a burning wall. But his real genius involved aircraft.

Contemporary newsreels show a tall, lean, broad-shouldered man with a droopy face, jug ears, a large nose, and a winning smile. Before a typical show, such as he performed at the 1935 Minnesota State Fair and at the Indiana State Fair's "Thrill Day" the following year, he wore white trousers, a dark sport coat, and a tie. The black-and-white footage shows a biplane taking off over the trees and fields alongside the fairground. The aircraft descends to about 8 feet off the ground, banks back and forth to straighten its path, then slams into a white frame "house," which has doors and windows to look authentic. When the biplane disappears into the roof, everything collapses except the front wall. A cloud of dust and splinters rises, and the plane appears demolished.

Frakes drew a crowd of more than 60,000 to the Iowa State Fair in 1937; 24,500 packed into the grandstand, and another 38,000 stood outside the track fence. Piloting a World War I plane that he'd bought in Fort Dodge for $500, Frakes was aware that federal and state officials were reportedly trying to stop his stunt. He took off from a wheat field east of town instead of the airport.

At the Indiana State Fair in 1938, he staged a midair collision, then upped the ante in 1939 by crashing into the roof of a barn-like building that he had rigged to catch fire (the lumber in the structure was already sawn halfway through). Flames erupted and firefighters hurried to the spot, just as Frakes emerged from the wreckage. He had nearly died during this stunt in 1937

when a fuel-soaked building collapsed and trapped him at the state fair in Oklahoma City in 1937. The crowd gasped as they watched him struggling to free himself. Firemen sprayed water at the burning structure, and Frakes finally got loose, his shirt and pants on fire, and minus one shoe. He suffered serious burns to his right hand, elbow, left arm, and his back. A fellow pilot who had been photographing the stunt from above was so sure that Frakes had been killed that he flew back to the airport, called the local newspaper, and offered photos of Frakes' final stunt.

By then, he had survived more than 50 crack-ups, and was nowhere near retiring. His next ploy was to rig the "houses" he crashed into with dynamite charges. One year he appeared at an Ohio State Fair that also featured a visit by Charles Lindbergh and a race between a biplane and an automobile. Frakes drew 60,000 spectators. He would spend 20 years smashing up aircraft, and would walk away from 100 crashes before retiring to Columbia, Tennessee.

Although the nail-biting exploits of Beachey, Frakes, and their peers made aircraft stunts a standard feature of

**Katherine Stinson poses by her aircraft at the Montana State Fair in 1913. Stinson was one of the best-known female aviation pioneers.** Montana Historical Society, Helena

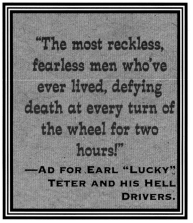

"The most reckless, fearless men who've ever lived, defying death at every turn of the wheel for two hours!"

—AD FOR EARL "LUCKY" TETER AND HIS HELL DRIVERS.

Stunt driver Marion Swanson slams through a wooden barrier at the Minnesota State Fair in 1934. Daredevil troupes were ever innovative in adding new acts to draw crowds, essaying all sorts of collisions, jumps, and rolls. Female drivers added to the appeal.
Minnesota Historical Society

fairs in the 1920s and 1930s, the public continually demanded variety. Capitalizing on the war in Europe, the 1941 Minnesota fair promised a demonstration of "the new aerial blitzkrieg," featuring attack planes, gliders, transports, parachute troops, and ground artillery. Parachute stunts had already declined (although, as late as 1951, the Alaska State Fair sponsored a particularly thrilling one in which the jumper got snagged on the plane's wingtip; his chute collapsed, but he managed to free himself and land safely). World War II gave the public a renewed interest in aircraft, but this would largely be a different sort of show—marked by high speed jets and tight formations. By the late 1930s, an article in *Popular Mechanics* pointed out, "The loop-the-loop artists and wing-walkers began to pall on the public . . . and auto poloists, human flies, high-wire walkers, and divers moved into the spotlight."

### CYCLES, CARS, AND TRAINS

Various wheeled vehicles had already been pressed into service as thrill-producers, even bicycles, an unlikely choice. In two accidents in the summer of 1902, bicyclists were seriously injured trying to loop the loop on special tracks; they lost control and pedaled off the ramp at the top of the loop. Later, bicyclists took to the high wire, where, equipped with long balance bars, they formed moving pyramids as they pedaled high above the grandstand infield. A contemporary photo caption called them "iron-nerved, death-defying aerialists."

Motorcycles were better suited to crowd-pleasing stunts because they were faster and noisier. Some motorcyclists smashed through walls of plate glass at top speed. Others raced around spherical, metal cages called motordromes.

As was the case with stunt pilots, female drivers in cars and on motorcycles got into the act. In 1934, Elfrieda Mazie, touted as "America's most famous woman daredevil," crashed her car through walls of flaming boards at speeds of 60 miles per hour. Driver Marion Swanson performed similar stunts at the time. In 1939, a female driver named Birdie Draper smashed her car through brick walls. Another female driver from the 1930s and star of the fair circuit was Marjorie Kemp, who called her troupe the Legion of Mad Speed Demons. Kemp raced around motordromes at 70 miles per hour with her pet lion Nero beside her. Kemp was one of the stars of Royal American Shows; a female daredevil named Ethel Purtle did a similar act for the World of Mirth carnival company. In the 1950s, Aut Swenson's Thrillcade featured Yvonne LaCosta, riding inverted on a wooden perch on top of a speeding car. In 1954, stunt woman Betty O'Day of the Royal American Shows reached speeds of 60 miles per hour in a motordrome, riding with her arms folded across her chest. Motorcycles, however, remained a mere footnote to the automobile, which soon took thrill shows to new heights of popularity. Among the most popular stunt drivers of his day was Earl "Lucky" Teter. At state fairs in the Midwest and the East in the 1930s, thrill hounds packed the grandstands to watch Teter and his Hell Drivers put on an action-packed hour of automobile crashes, races, and stunts. Advertisements called Teter a "world's champion daredevil" and his crew "The most reckless, fearless men who've ever lived, defying death at every turn of the wheel for two hours!"

Teter had been a test driver for carmakers before he discovered that smashing cars was both more fun and more lucrative. A creative showman, he was the first person to flip a car on purpose, according to some accounts. He justified his nickname on a regular basis, surviving numerous close calls. Fair promoter George Hamid, who knew him well, once watched Teter nearly drown after launching his car into a lake in Charlotte, North Carolina.

Audiences loved these feats, and Teter became a minor celebrity. When *Billboard* held a contest to gauge the most popular carnival and midway acts in 1939, Teter ranked 38th out of thousands in the list of top vote-getters.

Teter's advertisements were classics of their type, trumpeting hair-raising attractions. The "aerial crash" featured "A daring Hell Driver remaining inside a speeding car as it plunges off an incline rampway and noses into another automobile to depict one of the most horrible

**"From then on, it's a crashing, twisting, end-over-end mass of metal hurtling through the air."**
—AD FOR JOIE CHITWOOD AND HIS AUTO DAREDEVILS.

**Jimmie Lynch ups the ante by crashing through a wall that had been set afire, part of his "Death Dodgers" show at the Iowa State Fair's thrill day in 1939.**
State Historical Society of Iowa, Des Moines

automobile crashes ever conceived." Another stunt, "cyclone driving," involved "three Hell Drivers racing stock sedans up and down steep incline rampways, then criss-crossing in front of each other at a mile a minute."

Teter's crew at the 1936 New Jersey State Fair included such notables as "Suicide" Sanders, "Demon" Davis, "Fearless" Fern, "Daring" Daniel, and "Jumping" Jack Owen (the "World's champion motorcycle ski-jumper," ads said). They vaulted their cars over buses and rows of cars, crashed through tunnels of burning planks and explosives, and soared off ramps on motorcycles. Old newsreel footage shows a stunt during which a shirtless Hell Driver lay down in front of a small ramp; a huge truck then drove over him, barely missing his body. Teter's grand finale was usually an end-over-end, side-over-side somersault. When his car ended up inverted, a uniformed crew ran out to turn it back over.

59

**Hood already askew, a stunt driver gets some serious air at a Minnesota State Fair thrill day. The fair's first thrill day was in 1933; for three decades, the popular events packed the massive grandstand.**
Minnesota State Fair

(he won Eastern AAA championships in 1939, 1940, and 1942). He renamed the show the Auto Daredevils and raced off to fairground glory in the 1940s and 1950s.

Chitwood and his troupe played their first show on July 4, 1943, in Williams Grove, Pennsylvania. Chitwood had a knack for showmanship and business. By the time he appeared at the Nebraska State Fair in 1952, he had five units appearing at carnivals, race tracks, county and state fairs coast to coast, sometimes doing three shows a day.

Stunts included the "wingover," in which a car going 50 miles per hour raced up a ramp on the driver's side, ending up balancing on two wheels for 200 feet. In the "roll over," a car hurtled up a ramp that was high enough to flip it. "From then on," ads said, "it's a crashing, twisting, end-over-end mass of metal hurtling through the air." When two cars were destroyed during the show, Chitwood's crew piled one on top of the other, and then a

Tragedy struck at a benefit show for the Army Emergency Relief Fund on July 5, 1942, in front of the Indiana State Fair's grandstand. The 39-year-old Teter dedicated the show to the soldiers in the audience and to all the servicemen overseas. He talked of joining up, then announced that this show would be his last until the war ended.

Teter then donned his leather football helmet and joined his crew for the day's schedule of stunts, including one they'd done dozens of times, in which Teter would race up a wooden ramp and fly over a transport truck, landing on a second ramp. As he rounded a curve before starting up the first ramp, clouds of dust billowed around his car and perhaps clogged the carburetor. Witnesses heard the engine misfire. His car barely cleared the truck and smashed into the timbers supporting the second ramp. They cracked and broke, dropping the heavy ramp on Teter's car and pinning him beneath the wheel. He was dead on arrival at a local hospital.

Leaderless, the show nearly dissolved as Teter's widow put the equipment on the auction block. One of the Hell Drivers, Joie Chitwood, handled the sale as a favor to Teter's widow. He found no buyers, however, so he borrowed $20,000 and bought the outfit himself. Chitwood, a 200-pound, full-blooded Cherokee, had joined the team two years earlier. He was well-suited to his trade, having the aggressiveness of a former football player, the mechanical know-how of a former welder, and the behind-the-wheel savvy of a veteran dirt track driver in the Midwest and East

**Joie Chitwood appeared at the Delaware State Fair in 1964, along with other acts, including radio/television host and entertainer Arthur Godfrey and pop star Bobby Vinton.** Delaware State Fair

The locomotives will be "enveloped in flames with clouds of steam and smoke pouring from the battered hulks . . . a mass of mangled scrap iron."

—AD FOR LOCOMOTIVE COLLISION, MINNESOTA STATE FAIR, 1934.

On specially built tracks in front of state fair grandstands, two huge steam engines hurtled toward each other and oblivion. Dozens of such planned catastrophes drew gigantic crowds to fairs in the 1920s and 1930s, a time when fatal train wrecks were regular news. This locomotive collision headlined the Minnesota State Fair in 1934. Minnesota Historical Society

third old car raced up a ramp and pancaked on top of them—this stunt was called the Dive Bomber.

Shows also featured head-on collisions and 80-foot jumps on ramps that were just 5 feet high and 5 feet wide. A clown, "Crash" Roberts, pretended to wander into the path of oncoming cars and catch his foot in one of the wooden ramps. The speeding cars missed him by inches.

It had taken 50 stitches to close a gash on Chitwood's face—thanks to a stunt gone awry—when he spoke to Andrew Hamilton from *Popular Mechanics* magazine in 1951. The line between pretend accidents and real accidents was perilously thin. Asked about the qualifications for his trade, Chitwood explained: "Automobile stunting requires a combination of

courage, precision planning and split-second timing. Courage is a fine thing—but you can't get very far on nerve alone."

The interview offered a behind-the-scenes look at the business of auto thrill shows. Chitwood's teams drove late-model Ford stock sedans, with just three modifications. They removed the hubcaps, mounted a special metal apron on the front bumpers so they wouldn't gouge the wooden ramps, and put the gas tank inside the trunk.

His stable of drivers included veteran racer "Flash" Wardlow (a motorcyclist), stunt man "Snooks" Wentzell, and former circus performers. Another driver, Pierre Armand, had fought in the French resistance during World War II. A Hollywood scriptwriter couldn't have assembled a more swashbuckling crew.

In 1951, Chitwood's newest stunt was the "ice wall crash." A car equipped with rocket-like devices that spurted colored fire raced down a special track, setting off a series of dynamite caps before plowing into a large block of ice. Chitwood was also working on a ramp-to-ramp jump with a full twist in the air, a scheme that Teter had once outlined.

Competitors kept up the pressure to develop variations on old tricks or new spectacles. At state fairs in the 1950s, stunt driver "Irish" Horan shot a car (called "the Torpedobile") from a cannon. Others did ramp jumps in pickup trucks. The ramp jump was already a staple of thrill shows for decades; an early practitioner was Bud Toomey, who launched his sedan over 10 autos at the 1941 Minnesota fair. A steady stream of such stunts reached into the future. By the 1998 Iowa State Fair, second-generation stunt man Robbie Knievel was trying to jump 16 semi-tractor-trailers on his motorcycle. Knievel told reporters that his and his father's occupation was too dangerous, and that he didn't want his daughter (then 11) to do it. But he pointed out that his father had told him the same thing, and he hadn't listened.

No vehicle was safe from the creative eyes of stunt men and women, and even trains got in on the action. As early as 1896, massive audiences had gathered to witness one of the truly bizarre stunts mounted for the pleasure of fairgoers: the locomotive collision. Typically, a special track, several thousand feet long, would be laid on the grandstand infield; at each end would be a huge black locomotive, spewing tall plumes of white steam. Sometimes the engines pulled a coal car and a passenger car. The engineers started the locomotives on their fatal path, then stepped off. The collision produced a huge cloud of black smoke, which mixed with the steam that spouted from the mangled engines. The locomotives bucked off the tracks and telescoped together. Flames sometimes erupted from the cars.

Although—according to a local newspaper account from 1900—a collision "sent the crowd into bedlam with some spectators firing pistols and others crying loudly," the early locomotive collisions occurred at speeds of only 20 or 30 miles per hour (each locomotive going 10–15 miles per hour). Often the result was less than spectacular because the locomotives were too slow and too light, and the track was too short. By 1934 the Minnesota fair organizers had inclined the railroad tracks, upping the ramming speed to 60 miles per hour. Pre-fair promotions promised that, after this crash, the locomotives would be "enveloped in flames with clouds of steam and smoke pouring from the battered hulks . . . a mass of mangled scrap iron."

The master of the locomotive collision was "Head On" Joe Connolly, a native son of Iowa. During his 36-year career, he destroyed 146 locomotives in shows across the nation. The first, in 1896, and last, in 1932, were at the Iowa State Fair. The first wreck involved a pair of 41-ton locomotives that hit at a speed of 35 miles per hour, considered a high speed at the time. The spectacle drew a crowd of 55,000, including freeloaders who watched from a nearby hill and the tops of buildings.

The last crash, on a 3,000-foot track, was between locomotives named the Hoover and the Roosevelt, in honor of the two presidential candidates. At 112 tons, the engines were twice as big as the 1896 versions. A crowd of 45,000 showed up for the event; the collision was delayed an hour while police pushed back the crowd. Then the engineers and firemen propped open the throttles, tied down the whistle cords, and jumped off. The huge locomotives smashed into each other at about 50 miles per hour. The front couplers on the engines had been loaded with dynamite that exploded on impact. Two or three people in the audience were injured, including a woman on her honeymoon who was hit in the head with a piece of wood. The wreckage burned for several days.

## POLES, WIRES, AND PLATFORMS

Fair thrill shows didn't necessarily involve the roar of engines or the screech of twisting metal. High-wire acts often appeared at state fairs after the turn of the century, sometimes including elements of humor or surprise. At a show in 1902, a man wearing heavy rubber boots, a long

**The 1920 locomotive collision at the Minnesota State Fair had disappointed crowds; this photo was made in 1921, when the stunt was much more satisfactory. "It was a better collision than last year," a spectator observed, and it produced "a huge mass of twisted, steaming steel junk."** Minnesota State Fair

"THE GREAT TRAIN WRECK"
GRANDSTAND EVENT
MINNESOTA STATE FAIR-1921

overcoat, and a slouch hat climbed the 100-foot pole at one end of the wire. He pretended to stumble and fall as he walked out onto the wire, drawing gasps and laughs from the crowd far below. He then shed his outer garments, revealing the typical tight suit of the wire walker. He strolled to the middle of the wire, made up a bed, laid down, and pretended to go to sleep.

Human cannonballs sometimes shared the bill with high-diving horses—a famous one from the 1920s, named Kiawatha, dove 40 feet into a tank 8 feet deep, with a girl riding on his back. Diving animals got off comparatively easy; for them, any sort of jump was noteworthy. Their human counterparts had to work harder. In the 1930s, fire diver Jimmy Jamison wowed 'em with an 80-foot backward dive into a tank that was 6 feet deep and 15 feet across, covered with flames leaping 10 feet in the air. The descent took 1.5 seconds. When he hit the water feet first, the splash put out the flames. Thanks to an intense schedule of performances (he did the stunt three times a day for 16 weeks at an exposition in Chicago in 1934), by the end of the decade, Jamison had leaped into the burning tank 3,000 times, falling more than 60 miles through the air.

Jamison's female counterpart was Bee Kyle, winner of the 1939 *Billboard* contest mentioned above. Kyle's specialty was a back dive from 100 feet into a pool of water covered with burning gasoline.

Another popular high-rise stunt was the "sway pole," a single, tall, flexible mast that served as a platform. The performer set the pole swaying back and forth in larger and larger arcs, then dangled from a single stirrup.

Fair organizers sometimes erected the pole in front of the midway to attract crowds. In 1939, for example, Arzeno Selden (who called himself "the Stratosphere Man") did handstands on a 130-foot sway pole, and teetered on a kitchen chair from a lower perch, 90 feet off the ground. Selden had been a circus trapeze artist for 30 years before taking to the state fair circuit. He ended his show by biting onto a strap and sliding down a 500-foot rope to the ground, where he took his bows.

The Nebraska State Fair in 1954 featured a performer high in the air, but not someone on a pole or a wire. He was 57-year-old Ramon "Buddy" LaRue of Miami, a muscular, 135-pounder, sporting a thin mustache, a black beret, and a jersey that had his name written upside down in large letters. LaRue's name was inverted because his stunt involved dangling head downward from a cable beneath a helicopter, wearing a straitjacket. As the helicopter hovered over the grandstand, LaRue wriggled out of the jacket and dropped it to earth. "At first the CAA [Civil Aeronautics Authority] refused to

> "The loop-the-loop artists and wing walkers began to pall on the public . . . and auto poloists, human flies, high-wire walkers, and divers moved into the spotlight."
> —ARTICLE IN *POPULAR MECHANICS*, 1930S.

A fearless steed takes the plunge at the Utah State Fair, October 6, 1909. Sideshow promoters also trained dogs, elk, and pigs to leap into tanks of water. Used by permission, Utah State Historical Society, all rights reserved

approve the venture," a contemporary magazine article said, "but finally gave in on condition that he would put up $300,000 insurance for bystanders" (presumably because he might fall on them and they'd sue the fair). He had tried the stunt at a fairground in Milwaukee the previous June. His biggest worry, he said, was that the helicopter engine might conk out. "If that happens, I have an arrangement with the pilot to sort of swipe me sideways along the grass rather than let the ship crash down on me," he told a magazine writer. He was assuming that his pilot would remain coolheaded while riding a crashing helicopter to earth. Perhaps that was why LaRue gave him half of the $500 he earned per show.

And if the engine had conked out, the audience—like thrill show crowds everywhere—would have loved every second of it.

# CHAPTER FIVE

# The Greatest Sporting Event of the Year

At the end of the day, when the dust has settled and the sun has set, the most efficient farmer is the one who harnessed the most speed and power. Working the soil demands both, and without either, precious time is lost or critical tasks go undone. Power and speed, at their extremes, have also been a source of enduring fascination, prompting contests of swiftness and strength throughout history. At the agricultural fairs, these were contests of horses and horsepower.

Having the strongest or the fastest horse was a badge of honor that gave both owner and horse enviable reputations in the community. At the early fairs, spectators enjoyed plowing contests, in which the most powerful horses and their drivers competed against the clock and a plot of untilled land. The fastest horses went racing, a popular attraction since the Revolution, and a natural event at fairs. In time, cars and motorcycles would eclipse horses for speed and power and usher in new thrills for new generations of spectators.

In the 1840s and 1850s, plowing contests were the main events at rural fairs and gatherings, and the source of tremendous prestige to the winner. As the publication *Farmers' Cabinet* observed in 1841, "The immense concourse of persons who assembled together on the second day of the Exhibition of the Philadelphia Agricultural Society, to witness the trial of plows, showed very clearly the intense interest with which the subject was viewed by all classes; indeed, there is no object which at the present time is at all comparable with it in novelty, usefulness, or general importance." Even President Millard Fillmore visited the Baltimore Agricultural Fair in 1853 to watch a plowing match, officially recognizing the importance of the plow to a nation eager to develop its new territory by tilling the prairie.

Farmers were judged for both the speed of their work and the consistency of their furrows. The usual plot was a quarter acre, with categories for depth of the furrow (typically 6 inches and 10 inches) and for whether the farmer used horses or oxen. Each had its proponents. At the 1851 Wisconsin State Fair, a reporter noted, "a pair of working oxen owned by Mr. Jackman of Janesville excited a good deal of admiration by the rapid manner by which they got over the ground during the plowing match." Winning times varied dramatically, depending on the local soil: a winner at the Wisconsin fair took less than 30 minutes, whereas the winner at the Ohio State Fair (which held its first plowing contest in 1857) took half as long.

Plowing matches were a visible, influential test for the implement that was the keystone of a successful farm. Fairs continued the matches into the tractor era. The Iowa State Fair, which started holding plowing matches in 1907, sent the state's 4-H club winners on to a national contest. In 1953 a 16-time winner from Cherokee County (who described plowing as "a science and art combined") won the

> "It was not long before the horse race and the trotting match assumed an importance not entirely warranted on scientific grounds."
>
> —ESSAYIST FOSTER RHEA DULLES, IN *MASS LEISURE*, 1958

Harness racers raise dust in front of the grandstand at the 1904 Utah State Fair. Even when the other facilities were spartan, most fairs found the time, energy, and funds to build a track and a grandstand.

State **FunSpot 70** Fair
OF VIRGINIA
Richmond • Sept. 25 - Oct. 4

STATE FAIR
MAGAZINE

state contest, losing the national plowing contest in Wisconsin by a fraction of a point.

Plowing contests were orderly, methodical affairs, of interest only to the dwindling numbers of farmers who understood and appreciated the task. These contests lacked the color, noise, and excitement needed to draw the big crowds required by big fairs. Strong horses and careful drivers were fine in their own way; fast horses and ardent jockeys, however, were endlessly fascinating.

Since horses were the main source of transportation throughout the 19th century, speed and stamina had always been as valuable as strength. Thus, the plowing contest was supplemented by the speed trial. Both were necessary to document the advantages of careful breeding, practiced by growing numbers of farmers to improve their stocks of domesticated animals. This scientific purpose was alloyed with more

worldly desires. Journalist Phil Stong, describing the Puritans and Quakers, noted: "Once landed on their own territory they could not race horses for sport but they could 'improve the breed' . . . If it is more fun to have fun and call it 'improvement' why should anyone quibble? Improvement occurs."

After the Civil War, the plowing contest began to fade as a main attraction. Horse racing replaced it, becoming the "greatest sporting event of the year," and, for many fairgoers, the main reason for attending fairs. The surging popularity of horse racing built on a long tradition in the former colonies. With fast horses imported from England, races had been the principal sport before the Revolution, particularly in the large cities of the East. In one-time Puritan New England, trotting matches drew crowds of 30,000 to the Boston Agricultural Club.

When the starter's bell clanged and the horses bolted from the gate, excitement built among crowds of even the most taciturn farmers. The horses pounded around the final turn, manes flying in the wind, muscles rippling. Jockeys yelled "Hi! Hi!" and the crowds shouted, "Here they come!" The voice of the announcer gathered urgency, and the red, blue, and green silks of the drivers or jockeys ebbed and flowed. The vivid scene set the heart pounding and the blood racing.

Everywhere, it seemed, excited crowds gathered to watch harness races, speed races (in which horses ran half-mile, three-quarters, seven-eighths, and mile heats), and the steeplechase. Many fans liked the trotters and pacers;

Races involving camels and ostriches (top) were sheer gimmicks, amusing but of fleeting popularity. Horse races and auto races were serious attractions, even when betting wasn't allowed. Note that a demolition derby was an event at this state fair in the Old Dominion. State Fair of Virginia

This postcard shows the race track at the Eastern States Exposition, the "Fastest half-mile track in New England," according to text on the back. "Most of world's half-mile dirt track records made here," it adds. The bottom photo shows the Exposition's ample parking lots, which (the postcard promised) would hold 10,000 cars. Eastern States Exposition

RACE TRACK AND GRANDSTAND, EASTERN STATES EXPOSITION, SPRINGFIELD, MASS.

others preferred thoroughbreds. Mules, ponies, even burros (at a New Mexico State Fair) got into the act with events of their own.

Horse races and show rings drew larger and larger audiences at Eastern and Western fairs. By the 1867 New Jersey State Fair, horse races were described as "inevitable." Crowds numbering in the thousands watched from wooden grandstands or from their buckboards and buggies tied beside the race track fence, often eating picnic lunches as they sat. Farmers and city-dwellers alike were entranced; as a writer for *Scribner's* magazine observed in 1902, what "they both prefer at the fair is the trotting," which, he calculated, "drew ninety-hundredths of the crowd away from the other attractions."

When Indiana built a new fairground in 1891, promoters trumpeted that one attraction would be a "first-class mile track"; a sporting publication called *Western Horseman* announced that "Indiana will not only have the greatest fair . . . but Indianapolis will become one of the greatest trotting and pacing centers in the country." Race fans met this claim with enthusiasm. Six years later, 1,200 $1 seats were reserved in the grandstand for a three-heat

race, two days before the fair started. They wanted to see fast horses, and the names of a few became legend.

When a stylish, striking pacer named Dan Patch first attracted attention at county fairs in Indiana, savvy horsemen immediately knew that they were seeing the kind of animal that arrived once in a lifetime. Sired in Oxford, Indiana, in 1896, he was so superior to his supposed competition that he would lose only two heats in his entire career (and even then he won the overall races), remaining undefeated in three seasons of competition. His owners then settled on a series of speed exhibitions because Dan was so widely regarded as unbeatable that no one would ever bet against him.

This fair bill from the 1886 Ohio State Fair mentions the "New Fairgrounds" and its half-mile track. The center headline was of primary interest to numerous fairgoers who came strictly for the racing. Ohio Expositions Commission and C. LaVon Shook

A trotter and a runner grace the cover of this 1941 program from the California State Fair. The soldier at upper-right serves notice that war was upon us. Most state fairs were soon closed for the duration of hostilities. Those that persisted emphasized patriotic themes. California State Fair

The list of prizes for the 1885 Minnesota State Fair documents that race purses sometimes exceeded those for regular livestock, prompting critics to complain that horse races were taking over the fairs.
*Minnesota State Fair*

Whether the attraction was trotters, pacers, or (as shown here) runners, horse races at fairs were intensely popular and lucrative. This poster was for the horse show at the Springfield Fair, one of the former names of the Eastern States Exposition.
*Eastern States Exposition*

Gamblers may have been disappointed, but the formula worked well. During his peak years, the horse billed as "Dan Patch, the Pacing Wonder" traveled with four grooms who wore white, and rode from track to track in a private, white rail car. State fairs paid thousands of dollars for the exhibitions, then made back their investment tenfold as mammoth crowds jammed the grandstands for a glimpse.

He paced his first 2:00 mile in 1902, followed by a 1:59.5 in 1903, a year in which he also recorded a 1:56.25 with a bike sulky, and a 1:57.25 with a wagon. He chalked up a 1:55.25 in his last race, in 1905. At the Indiana State fair that year, 30,000 people (including 5,000 who camped overnight on the track's infield) had watched to

For some fans, harness racing was the only kind worth watching. When the Indiana State Fair was building its track, local people debated whether the track should hold sulky-carriage races ("the people's race horse," as one commentator put it) or races for runners ("the gambler's race horse"). Eamswood Communications, Inc., for the State Fair of West Virginia

"Once landed on their own territory they could not race horses for sport but they could 'improve the breed.' If it is more fun to have fun and call it 'improvement' why should anyone quibble? Improvement occurs."
—PHIL STONG, DESCRIBING QUAKER AND PURITAN ATTITUDES TOWARD HORSE RACING.

The flash of colored jerseys, the muffled drumbeat of pounding hooves, the excited voice of the announcer—for generations, these elements combined to produce the pinnacle of the state fair experience for some folks. Iowa State Fair, Des Moines

**SOUTHERN OHIO FAIR GROUNDS AT DAYTON**
AS THEY APPEARED FRIDAY OCT. 2° 1874 GOLDSMITH MAID AND MATE ON THE TRACK

The Ohio State Fair of 1874 was held in Dayton, and attendance was obviously excellent. The men in the foreground are standing on the paddock. At a state fair two years earlier, a visitor had written, "Soon after dinnertime the amphitheater, and the space on each side of the track . . . was packed by a dense throng of people, on foot and in carriages, drawn thither . . . by the report that some fast horses on the Trotting Park Course would be entered."
Ohio Expositions Commission and C. LaVon Shook

see if Dan Patch could run the Fair's first two-minute mile. A wet track foiled the attempt. The horse's fastest mile, a 1:55 behind a dirt shield at the Minnesota State Fair in 1906, wasn't recognized by racing officials, but this record stood for more than 50 years.

The runaway popularity of horse racing brought controversy. At California state fairs in the 1880s, races drew crowds of 15,000, generating complaints from state chapters of the Grange about the overemphasis of horse racing. Critics pointed out that the purses for winning horses were twice the total of all other premiums combined. Purses and prizes of several thousand dollars were common at races in the 1860s and 1870s. Complaints about the concentration on horse racing at agricultural fairs had been heard before the Civil War. Invariably, however, objections were rebutted by the fact that horse races made money and increased attendance, two things no fair manager scoffed at.

When the Illinois State Fair banished horse races during the mid- and late 1860s, half the fairgoers stayed home. Brief periods of popular disapproval of horse racing—such as during the Civil War, triggered by rampant commercialism, gambling, and cheating—were brief, and the sport rebounded, rapidly reaching even greater heights of popularity.

The Texas State Fair survived when the state legislature banned gambling on horse races in 1902, although it lost one of its chief attractions and its main source of income (betting on horse races was again legalized in 1934, and celebrated with a new race track complex). In New Jersey, the state fairs had largely been paid for by horse racing starting in 1867. The fairs failed when the state legislature banned gambling in 1899.

A typical complaint, concerning the Pennsylvania State Fair at Philadelphia in 1856, appeared in the *Philadelphia Ledger.* "There is danger that agricultural fairs may be ruined by transforming them into race courses." As historian Wayne

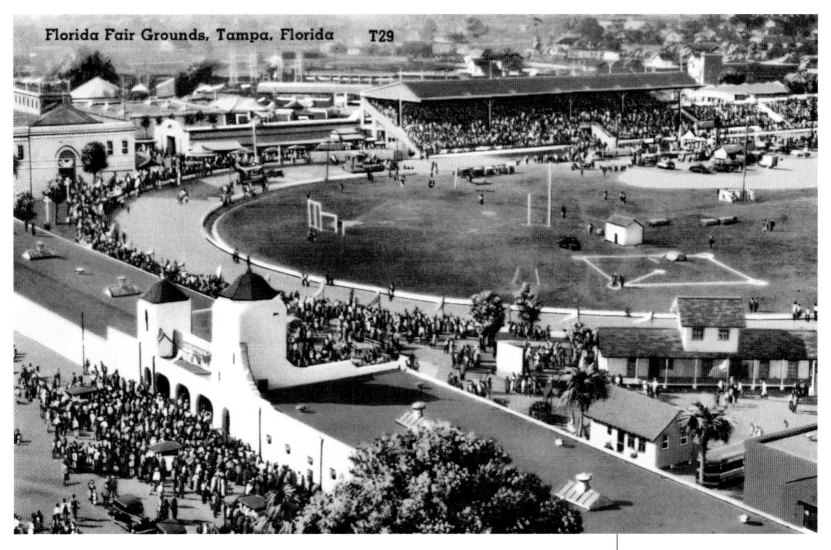

Florida Fair Grounds, Tampa, Florida    T29

Neely noted, "Many of the fairs came into the hands of jockey clubs and sporting associations . . . many of them lost a considerable measure of popular support."

Actually, a number of fairs owed their origins to racing. The grounds of the Maine State Fair in Lewiston had been owned by the Androscoggin Trotting Society, which operated a horse track. In 1906 the Tennessee State Fair used Cumberland Park, where the Cumberland Park Fair and Racing Association had held harness races. The Maryland Jockey Club owned the fairgrounds used by the Maryland State Fair in the early 1900s. In Arizona, J. C. Adams, the first chairman of the Fair Commission and the Fair Association, was described as "a zealous owner of race horses, and especially of pacers and trotters."

Although horses were wonderfully popular, they didn't keep the field all to themselves as an attraction. In the first decade of the 20th century, a noisy, smoky, and dan-gerous competitor appeared, one that could go twice as fast. Where the race horse represented tradition, the racing automobile represented the modern era.

A car racing craze swept the country in the first decade of the new century. At some fairs, horses and cars shared a dirt track. One year, the Iowa State Fair featured five days of horse racing, two days of auto racing, and six days of whippet racing. At the Arizona fairgrounds in 1912, the existing mile horse track was given a hard surface and banked turns, and handed over to car racers. Soon, Dan Patch had famous two-legged counterparts in drivers like Barney Oldfield and Eddie Rickenbacker.

Berna Eli Oldfield had been a champion bicycle racer before taking up automobile racing. Oldfield drove the world's first one-minute mile in a race at the Indiana fairground in June 1903. By 1909 he was a household name, thanks to a grueling schedule of races and time trials that

**A race track is a prominent feature in this view of the old Florida fairground in Tampa, built in 1904. This Southern fair had several names during its early incarnations, including the South Florida Fair (1904) and the South Florida Fair and Gasparilla Carnival (1915). Originally held on a two-acre plot in downtown Tampa near the University of Tampa, it moved to its current 319-acre home in 1976.**

# DAN PATCH

DAN PATCH 1:55

Set World Record of 1:55 in 1906 at The
Minnesota State Fair On a One Mile Track

In 1905 Dan Patch was arguably the biggest sports hero in America, and possibly the best-known celebrity of any kind during that era. Typical of his drawing power was a visit to the Indiana State Fair in 1905 (he was then nine years old), when he drew a crowd of 30,000 to the track's old amphitheater.
Minnesota State Fair

spanned the nation. In a two-year stretch, Oldfield raced against time or competition as often as three times a week. In 1910 he reached an astonishing 131 miles per hour in a German Blitzen Benz. Driving what was probably the first race car subsidized by a car maker, Henry Ford's famous No. 999, Oldfield did a mile in 49 seconds at the Minnesota State Fair track in 1918. He remained a popular figure long after his competitive days ended, racing tractors as promotional stunts at fairs across the Midwest. At the Indiana State Fair in 1933, for example, he drove an Allis-Chalmers tractor to what was termed "a world's tractor speed record" of 39 miles per hour.

Rickenbacker started his racing career at 16 and set numerous speed records. He also had some close calls. At

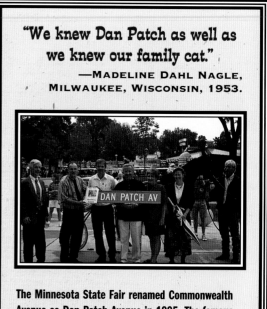

"We knew Dan Patch as well as we knew our family cat."
—MADELINE DAHL NAGLE, MILWAUKEE, WISCONSIN, 1953.

The Minnesota State Fair renamed Commonwealth Avenue as Dan Patch Avenue in 1995. The famous horse had been owned by native son M. W. Savage, and thus was a suitable figure for permanent commemoration at that state's fairground. Harness racing was a major attraction from the beginning of the Minnesota fair. Dan Patch first raced there in 1903. The fair's last horse races took place in 1949. Minnesota State Fair

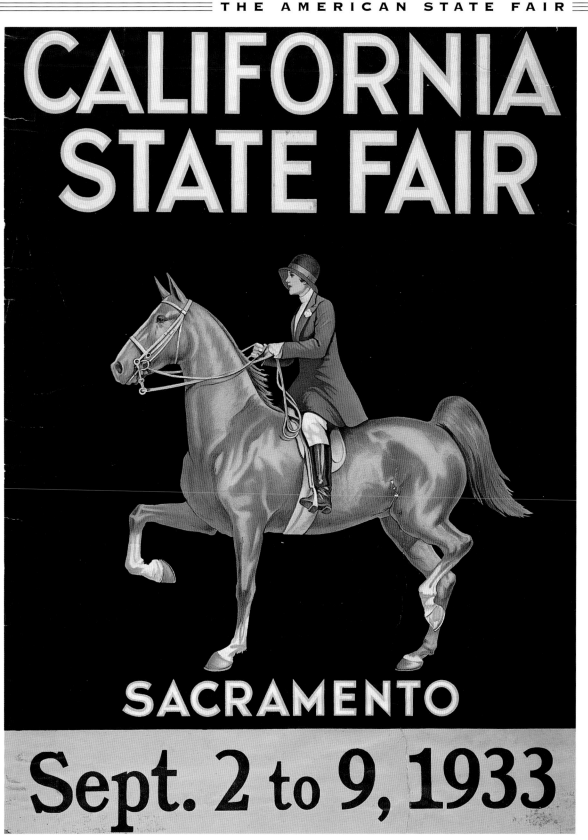

**Swen Peterson leads Ted Hartley through a turn at the 1932 Iowa State Fair.** State Historical Society of Iowa, Des Moines

**"There is danger that agricultural fairs may be ruined by transforming them into race courses."**
— *PHILADELPHIA LEDGER*, 1856.

During this tractor race at the 1933 Indiana State Fair, winner Barney Oldfield set a speed record of 39 miles per hour. Oldfield had retired from auto racing, but his famous name still filled the seats.
Indiana State Archives, Indiana Commission on Public Records, all rights reserved

Lincoln Beachey, who died in a stunt the following year, banks his biplane as he races Eddie Rickenbacker at the 1914 Iowa State Fair. Given Rickenbacker's legendary record as an ace in World War I, one might expect that he'd be the one in the airplane; however, he was a well-known auto racer as a young man. State Historical Society of Iowa, Des Moines

**"Nowadays the auto races are three times as popular as the trotters, for the artful speedsters have learned to go through fences without injury [and] are able to provide a breathtaking accident almost every race."**
— *ARTICLE IN TIME ON THE IOWA STATE FAIR,* 1935.

Not all winners at fairs got the coveted blue ribbons. The extravagant trophies for automobile races—and the sizable purses—matched the seriousness of the legions of fans. Minnesota State Fair

25¢

Auto racer Buzz McCain's battered helmet, displayed at the Minnesota State Fair's museum, shows that the sport wasn't necessarily non-contact. Minnesota State Fair

Car wrecks were the center of interest on the cover of this program from the 1961 Minnesota State Fair. Although fans were primarily interested in speed records, they were never averse to a few smash-ups. Minnesota State Fair

the Minnesota State Fair race track one year, his car careened off the track and flipped. He wasn't wearing a safety belt and bounced out when the car slammed into the ground, but he escaped serious injury. Rickenbacker went on to greater glory by becoming the leading American flying ace of World War I.

Just as great horses, such as the trotter Greyhound, were compared to predecessors like Dan Patch, so too were the best drivers. Auto racer Gus Schrader was often mentioned in the same breath with Oldfield. Engaging in well-publicized duels with such rival racers as Emory Collins, contesting for the national dirt-track championship, Schrader was a huge draw at fairs. At the Minnesota State Fair in 1941, when Schrader (who had been world dirt-track champion for eight of the previous nine years) talked of making that fair his farewell appearance, reporters noted that he was, at 46, two years older than the "great Barney Oldfield," who had been the first champion. Schrader, a headline attraction at the fair, held most of the world records on half-mile tracks at distances from one-half to 25 miles. Oldfield had once entered the record books with a mile track record at the Arizona State Fair of 48 seconds; Schrader's one-mile record was 24.44 seconds, set at the 1940 Minnesota fair.

A huge variety of races and speed events evolved, including 100-milers. One such race, begun in the 1920s, featured what contemporary accounts called the "Midwest's greatest Negro pilots," under the auspices of the Indianapolis Colored Auto Racing Association. In a grueling 1932 race, the field of 26 starters dwindled to just 7 finishers.

As in most other realms of competition, female speedsters such as Joan LaCosta ("hailed as the greatest woman driver the world has ever seen," a promotion said) got into the act. LaCosta once hit 145 miles per hour on a straightaway in Florida. When she appeared at the Iowa fair in the 1920s, articles about her pointed out that she held the women's mile dirt-track record, 45.5 seconds, within three seconds of the men's time.

Early car races had often featured a heat just for Fords, a nod to the dominant automaker of the time. By Schrader's day, the automotive line-up was considerably more varied. A typical race bill, from 1941, featured drivers Phil Mocca and Shorty Burns driving Cragars, Schrader and Jimmie Wilburn in Offenhausers, and other contestants behind the wheels of Hispano-Suizas, Miller Specials, and Gerber Specials.

Although raw speed was no doubt the chief lure of auto racing, the constant threat of crashes was an undeniable attraction as well. As a 1935 article in *Time* noted, referring to that year's Iowa State Fair, "Nowadays the auto races are three times as popular as the trotters, for the artful speedsters have learned to go through fences without injury [and] are able to provide a breathtaking accident almost every race."

Drivers earned reputations for their fearlessness and risk taking, but the results weren't always harmless. When the Indiana State Fair tried out a 100-mile race, a driver died when he hit a concrete bridge tunnel. Auto races there were canceled until the mid-1950s.

Another mishap presaged modern problems with the paparazzi. At the Minnesota State Fair in 1953, before a crowd of more than 11,000, a driver's wheels locked in a turn. He slammed into the wall, caromed back and flipped. Track officials and press photographers clashed as the latter raced out to take photos. Editors

knew such photos were sure-fire; readers enjoyed reading about wrecks as much as spectators liked watching them.

Auto polo, a peculiar combination of contest and exhibition, had already capitalized on this desire. At many state fairs starting around 1915, contestants drove stripped-down Model T Fords equipped with roll bars and a special framework over the radiator. In one version, one man drove while another wielded a standard polo mallet. In another type of auto polo, drivers bumped 6-foot balls toward goal posts, blocking, ramming, and sideswiping each other en route. Promotional stories emphasized the quick, sharp turns demanded by the event, and, of course, speed. "Spills and upsets are frequent," an ad said.

With typical exaggeration, a newspaper advertisement called auto polo "the most exciting game ever staged by humans," printing the accolade along with a photo of a collision in which one car had overturned. A regular season of auto polo between two teams produced 1,500 broken axles, and flat tires by the dozen each week.

Gradually, this odd event may have transformed itself into what we now know as the demolition derby. An intermediate step in the evolution was what the 1951 Nebraska State Fair (featuring driver Aut Swenson and his Thrillcade) called a "crash roll tournament." In this event, contestants scored points each time they did a complete rollover, eventually demolishing their cars. Another novelty act that appeared at fairs during the same era was

troupes of chimpanzees driving miniature race cars. They invariably ended up in what ads called "a riotous snarl."

Former racer and longtime demolition derby promoter Dutch Holland isn't sure when demolition derbies began; he got into the sport in the 1960s, after spending a decade racing on dirt and paved tracks. His original partner had been driving in demolition derbies since the 1940s, Holland believes.

When Holland started, his car of choice was a 1957 or 1958 Mercury. He describes it as a "box type" car, very heavy with strong bumpers. Staying with one make and model let drivers easily interchange parts, an obvious necessity. He remembers paying $25 for used cars, including one that a farmer was using as a chicken coop—"It was full of chickens," Holland recalls, "and it took a lot of hard work to clean it up." He demolished 17 of these vehicles in one year.

A typical season for Holland included 25 or 30 events, a schedule he followed for 10 years, injury-free. In the early days, the last car running was the winner. Now judges give points for gutsiness and aggressiveness, so that drivers don't just lay back in the early stages. Modern demolition derbies feature motorcycles, trucks, even combines, a surprising development in a series of events that started with horses pulling a plow. Horses raced, then cars raced, then cars wrecked each other on purpose. Now combines slam away at each other.

The next step is unpredictable, but whatever it is, excited crowds at fairs will no doubt have the chance to find out.

Demolition-derby promoter Dutch Holland got into the sport in the early days as a contestant. Here are before and after shots from a typical meet in El Centro, California, in the 1960s; cars roared in backward to protect their engines. Today, Holland's three crews perform at the California and Nevada state fairs, as well as several dozen smaller agricultural fairs in California.
Dutch Holland

79

# CHAPTER SIX

# An Avalanche of Attractions

In 1800, entertainment was a sin. When 20 million visitors flocked to the World's Columbian Exposition at Chicago in 1893, it had become mainstream.

Fairs had always included minor amusements, but in Chicago, the myriad shows, stunts, novelties, displays, games, contests, food stands, and carnival rides filled a gaudy, mile-long strip. Several ethnic villages were on display, the most popular being a simulated street from Cairo where mostly male crowds eyeballed exotic dancers. Strange animals, a strong man, and magician Harry Houdini appeared on other stages. Visitors could also view a stuffed horse billed as the only survivor of Custer's last stand (what they meant was "the only survivor of the federal forces," but it would be decades before native Americans, whose ancestors won that battle, could have effectively challenged the original description). Visitors with pockets full of coins could play games, listen to recorded music, and peer at mildly naughty peepshows in booths of "automatic" amusement machines. The Ferris wheel, which remains emblematic of fairs and carnivals after a century, was introduced in Chicago, where it was the only attraction that outdrew the swiveling midriffs of the exotic dancers.

The Columbian Exposition was much more than a state fair, but its amusement center—the Midway Plaisance—was the archetype of the countless smaller midways that became mandatory features of state fairs, thereby adding the word "midway" to the American vernacular. By the 1904 World's

"[W]ho shall compute the tintype galleries, bamboo slides, penny vaudevilles, sand-bumps, graphophones, merry-go-rounds, strength-testing devices, nickel-in-the-slot machines, Japanese 'gambling' games, rifle-ranges, and establishments where 'you get your money back if I fail to guess your weight within three pounds'?"

—FROM *THE PEOPLE AT PLAY*, BY AMUSEMENT HISTORIAN ROLLIN HARTT, 1909.

Fair in St. Louis, the midway had completed its transformation from what had begun, literally, as "sideshows," relegated to the margins of a fair (or banished altogether). The St. Louis midway was located in the heart of the fairground.

Fairs everywhere, large and small, used midways to attract larger crowds. The Arizona State Fair called its midway the Joy Zone; Minnesota's was the Merry Pike. In his 1909 book, *The People at Play*, Rollin Hartt wrote: "The mardigras, the fiesta, the penny vaudeville, the circus, the dime museum, and the jubilant terrors of Coney Island, were rifled of their magic. Never was the Midway so frantic, so extravagant, so upsetting, so innocuously bacchanalian!"

The carnivals that enlivened fair midways were the vagabond descendants of early "amusement parks" whose gardens and fountains served as a soothing backdrop for picnics and quiet strolls. Coney Island, the mecca of American diversion, transformed this bucolic setting. From 1886 to 1906, this five-mile sandbar at the foot of Brooklyn was the most famous resort in the world, setting the pace and style for the 2,000 amusement parks

**The combination of huge, lurid banners and gifted pitchmen proved almost irresistible for visitors on the grounds of the Vermont State Fair in 1941. However, as Scribner's magazine noted in August 1903, "The showmen themselves were far more entertaining than any performances they had to offer within their gates, and in their particular line they were wonders."** Jack Delano/Library of Congress, LC-USF35-47

**The "Strawberry Roan" state fair.**
Library of Congress, LC USZC2-3676

**What wonders await inside the shadowy sideshow? That was no doubt the question in the minds of these curious boys attending the Vermont State Fair in 1941.**
Jack Delano/Library of Congress, LC-USF35-42

that sprang up in the United States by 1909. Coney Island's antic innovations made amusement parks busier, noisier, wilder, and more surprising. Its name became synonymous with the midway's mechanical fun; in 1937, a writer could remark, "The midway blossoms with . . . Coney Island rides."

Amusement parks and carnivals borrowed their cartoon architecture from a dozen foreign lands; towers, domes, and cupolas appeared in a rainbow of colors and sprouted bright flags and banners. Musicians played outlandish music. Rides whirled and jostled shrieking passengers. Entertainers from Europe and Africa vied for attention.

Midways were packed with alluring sights and sounds. "Who shall number the beatific Moxie stands, the popcorn and peanut stalls, the rapturous candy-mills?" amusement historian Rollin Hartt rhetorically asked. These offerings mixed with dozens of other exhibits, games, and contests, challenging fairgoers' skill, strength, courage, and sometimes, gullibility.

Popcorn, the rifle range, the carousel, and the weight-guesser remain staples of fair midways after 90 years. The Ohio State Fair installed a weight-guesser in 1948; since then, a fair publicist once computed, the carnies who have manned the booth have guessed more than a billion pounds of weight. But a few of these antique attractions may be unfamiliar to modern readers. Moxie is a New England soft drink that was originally developed in 1884 as a patent nerve medicine for such complaints as "loss of manhood" and "softening of the brain." Shedding these spurious claims and adding carbonation around 1900, Moxie quickly became America's first mass-market soft drink. Graphophone was a trademark for an early phonograph that played wax records. Tintypes (also known as ferrotypes, a type of early photograph) were popular novelty mementos; a

Elephants from a circus parade decorate two of the letters on this postcard. Toward the end of their heyday in America, circus troupes found fairs to be ideal venues. Eventually, carnival companies took over the role.

The Midway Plaisance at the Montana state fairground, circa 1911. The ubiquitous Ferris wheel turns in the background. Sharp-eyed readers can spot a couple of cowboy hats in the dense crowd, but, in keeping with the times, most fairgoers were formally dressed. This photo was taken by Leslie Lyle of Helena. Montana Historical Society, Helena

These posters were produced and distributed by the carnival company rather than the fair itself, thus their emphasis on the midway was understandable. Eamswood Communications, Inc., for the State Fair of West Virginia

"ENTERTAINMENT IN THE GRAND STYLE!"

JAMES E. STRATES SHOWS

SIDE SHOW
JAMES E. STRATES
SHOWS

JAMES E. STRATES

FREE BAND
CONCERT

FEATURING
YOUNG STRANGLER LEWIS

STATE
FAIR

The goal of the James E. Strates Shows is being good at what we do and to take great pride in doing it. In the more than six decades of our operation, the vast storehouse of knowledge gained in the art of making a carnival is like no other. We have our own unique way of providing entertainment in the grand style. That, coupled with a profound sense of value and a burning desire to be the best, is the cornerstone of our operation. Our dedication to perfection, attention to detail, and devotion to quality manifests itself in our Show today. The seas of smiling faces, the shouts of laughter and eyes round with wonder are rewards that cannot be measured in the "coin of the realm." They are justly earned, and we intend to keep it that way.

James E. Strates

**James E. Strates Shows, America's only remaining railroad carnival, still rides the rails to its dates during a seven-month season on the East Coast, hauling 45 rides, 80 games and concessions, and a long heritage in the carnival business. The company's founder emigrated from Greece to America in 1909 when he was 15. He did odd jobs before joining a carnival athletic show, in which he wrestled all comers as "Young Strangler Lewis," pictured at lower left on the billboard in this drawing.** James E. Strates Shows

1903 issue of *Scribner's* magazine noted, "If you are a bachelor, sentimental and anxious to make a deep impression on a certain young woman, the vital question is not whether she wishes to see the latest style harvester or the Perry Brothers' exhibit of Plymouth Rocks. It is rather, does she want an orange or a tintype."

During the 18th century, the Puritans would have been scandalized by the frenzied midway scene. However, the restrictive religious doctrines that held music and theater to be sinful gradually began losing their hold on the majority of American citizens. In the 1830s, amusements that had no educational rationale drew larger and larger audiences. And by the 1840s and 1850s, it was clear even to opponents of commercial, secular amusements that entertainers were here to stay. Fairs, building on their serious, work-oriented foundation, quickly exhibited the effects.

Before entertainment could reach widespread public acceptance, it had to become respectable. Pioneering pitchmen quickly learned that they could exhibit nearly anything if they advertised it as educational and morally inspiring. The public went along with this sometimes transparent ruse, keeping the censors at bay. The result was a subtle blending of education and entertainment that took place in each of the events that were the midway's precursors: traveling lectures, feats of skill or daring, exhibits of curiosities, and huge murals called "panoramas." A motley assortment of traveling shows was already becoming concentrated into several specialized and popular events, including circuses, medicine shows (which sometimes offered small, unrelated shows for free as part of their pitch to attract customers— perhaps the earliest use of entertainment merely as a vehicle for the express delivery of advertising), and menageries.

Panoramas were a series of huge, painted murals that turned in sequential order in front of an audience. A European invention, these immense murals brought heroes, villains, disasters, battles, and landmarks to audiences that were largely rural, uneducated, and fascinated by the larger world outside their town. Other shows simulated trips on lakes and rivers, tours of London and Paris, scenes from the Revolutionary War, or views of important towns in the United States, often extolling the value of industry and the work ethic.

Panoramas traveled to hundreds of American towns between 1840 and 1860. State fairs were an excellent opportunity to find a large, willing audience. The lecturer stood in front of the mural, pointing out important items with a long stick. Some panoramas were based on current events. One 1857 show—"Dr. Kane's Arctic Expedition"—depicted the exploits of Elisha Kent Kane, an American doctor and explorer who sailed on record-setting Arctic expeditions in 1850 and 1853. When their ship became frozen in the ice, Kane led a harrowing overland retreat via Greenland. His resulting fame and premature death at age 37 made him an ideal subject.

The Indiana State Fair in 1888 featured a high-tech development called a cyclorama: a circular, stationary

**The guess-your-age booth is a surprisingly venerable attraction, here staffed by a mighty youthful carnie. References to age- and weight-guessers appear as early as 1909 in historical annals of fairs and carnivals. Folks are always happy to hear someone tell them that they look younger or lighter than they actually are, even if it costs them a nickel to win a penny prize.** Iowa State Fair, Des Moines

In spite of compliments about one's apparent youthfulness, most folks do in fact look their age (to a trained guesser, that is). This booth was an attraction at the 1946 Iowa State Fair. Iowa State Fair—Des Moines

"Watching the many rides, booths and stands go up with the auction tent was exciting all week long. The gaiety of people yelling at the races or screaming on the rides would fill the air until midnight."

—TAMYRA YAGEL, ORMOND BEACH, FLORIDA (SHE WAS BORN IN 1941 ACROSS THE STREET FROM THE MICHIGAN FAIRGROUND).

These lucky children got a memorable ride as part of the circus parade at an Indiana State Fair. Following circus tradition, fairs sometimes staged parades through downtown to drum up business.
J. C. Allen and Son, Inc.

panorama in front of which a seated audience rode on a mechanical conveyor. As Indiana fairgoers watched "The Battle of Atlanta," they saw the events that took place from May to September 1864, when Union troops gradually encircled and then bombarded the Georgia city that was the South's center for communications and supplies. Confederate troops abandoned the city on September 1; the following day, Union General W. T. Sherman occupied the city and burned it. The show was billed as "The Most Magnificent Cyclorama in the United States—Fifty Feet High, Four Hundred Feet in Circumference. 30,000 Soldiers in Action. Larger and Finer than the Famous Gettysburg, of Chicago."

Within a decade, fair audiences goggled at the next generation of spectacle, fireworks. Relying heavily on the imaginations of the audience, promoters mined world history for suitable disasters and cataclysms. They presented "The Last Days of Pompeii" (buried by the eruption of Mt. Vesuvius in 79 A.D.), and "The Burning of Chicago" (which killed several hundred and left 90,000 homeless in 1871). In 1927 the Iowa State Fair advertised "The Fall of Troy," complete with "scenic novelties . . . elaborate costuming, special lighting effects and a large cast of characters." Helen was abducted, Troy besieged. Actors built the famous wooden horse, and the show ended with the destruction of the city, attended by fireworks and "giant explosive effects." Other fairs capitalized on current events instead of history. At the outset of World War I, the Minnesota State Fair offered "The War of Nations," with aerial battles, the bombardment of a city, and the destruction of cathedrals.

The results didn't always match the hyperbole-filled advertisements. At the Indiana State Fair in 1898, a fireworks show entitled the "Battle of Manila," depicting Commodore George Dewey's destruction of the Spanish fleet during the Spanish-American War earlier that year, was found by audiences to be "tame." The Minnesota State Fair tried it the following year, with better results.

"If you are a bachelor, sentimental and anxious to make a deep impression on a certain young woman, the vital question is not whether she wishes to see the latest style harvester or the Perry Brothers' exhibit of Plymouth Rocks. It is rather, does she want an orange or a tintype."
—*SCRIBNER'S* MAGAZINE, 1903.

Growing ever more elaborate, the shows added elements of pageant and drama. The Indiana fair once featured "Hawaiian Nights," a "remarkable, vivid and realistic portrayal of life in the Island Home of Love and Romance," promoters said, featuring a cast of 300, the eruption of Mauna Loa, and the destruction of a village. In 1925 the fair offered "Cleopatra," a 500-foot-wide spectacle and fireworks show, with four dozen dancers and a ballet.

Fairs offered orchestral concerts and operas, water pageants and vaudeville. John Philip Sousa and his 70-piece orchestra ("easily the most outstanding musical attraction in North America," ads said) headlined several fairs in the 1920s. The Minnesota State Fair in 1935 presented what it called the State Fair Revue, featuring Radio City Music Hall dancers and minor Hollywood starlets. The nonstop entertainment, dramatic lighting, and grandiose action of these spectacles had long been standard for circuses, which also played dates at state fairs. A particular type of circus—the Wild West Show—brought a Lebanese immigrant named George Hamid into the world of American fairs and carnivals.

**Rodeos quickly became a mandatory feature of Western fairs. At huge state fairs they were elaborate; at smaller fairs, such as this one organized by homesteaders at Pie Town, New Mexico, they were much simpler. But in either case, once the bull left the chute, sheer excitement ensued.** Russell Lee/Library of Congress, LC-USF35-346

Rodeo is not the sole purview of the far West; it remains popular and highly competitive in the Midwest, as well. This cowboy is trying his luck at the 1966 Iowa State Fair. Iowa State Fair, Des Moines

in person
## EDDY ARNOLD
1969

FESTUS of GUNSMOKE

AND MANY OTHER GREAT STARS

## SEPT. 26-OCT. 5
ARKANSAS LIVESTOCK
## EXPOSITION

Hamid's long career (first as an acrobat and later as a major promoter and booking agent) began when he was nine years old. Hamid was then the junior member of an acrobatic troupe that had joined Buffalo Bill Cody's show in France. He and his brothers eventually headed for America, reaching Ellis Island in 1907. Perhaps prophetically, he spent his first night in America in a barn at a fairground in Hoboken, New Jersey.

In Lebanon, farmers tumbled as a hobby. Hamid figured acrobats would be popular in America, too, paired with the clowns who usually gave a free show in front of the grandstand. By 1919 his two acrobatic troops worked fairs all summer. Thirty years later, Hamid headed the country's largest booking agency for circuses and outdoor amusement acts; a contemporary writer called him the "undisputed king of the midway."

He handled 300 acts and was president of the New Jersey State Fair for several years.

Even Hamid's vast stable of performers represented but a fraction of the spectrum of entertainment that appeared at fairs: illusionists, snake handlers, flea circuses, jugglers, and trick dogs. The Wallenda family took their famous high-wire act to numerous state fairs in the 1950s. There were foot races, baseball and football games. Dogs did tricks. Trained mules and unicyclists did comedy routines. Clowns strolled the midway with pet skunks.

An organ-grinder named Harry Richards, who lived in a trailer with his monkeys, appeared at the Santa Clara (California) County Fair in the 1950s. Fair manager Russell Pettit charged Richards the usual fee until he found out that the state fair paid Richards to perform. "Now I let him work for free, because he and his spry little monkeys delight small fry and oldsters alike," Pettit told a writer for the *Saturday Evening Post.* "Organ grinders are becoming as scarce as buggy whips."

The Wild West show, which gave George Hamid his first job, had a long run as a fair attraction, with trick riding, roping, costume dramas, and a host of other surprising elements. At the Indiana State Fair in 1928, A. C. Rowland's Flying X Rodeo featured 25 male and female cowboys, a 10-piece band, a herd of 150 wild horses from Montana, and 15 Indians. In his pitch to the fair managers, Rowland offered to bring a live buffalo. Cowboys would ride it every day; the Indians would kill it during a mock-hunt on the next-to-last day of the fair. Then

In 1927, when composer John Philip Sousa appeared at the Iowa State Fair with his 70-piece band, fair promoters could confidently announce that Sousa and his band were "easily the most outstanding musical attraction in North America." Forty years later, as this poster attests, popular tastes in music had changed, and fairs sought out stars to appeal to younger audiences. Arkansas State Fair

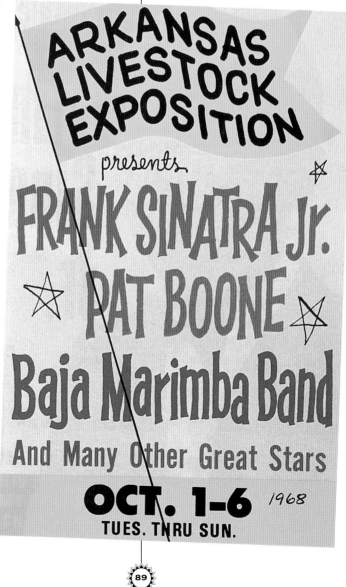

ARKANSAS
LIVESTOCK
EXPOSITION

presents

## FRANK SINATRA Jr.
## PAT BOONE
## Baja Marimba Band
And Many Other Great Stars

## OCT. 1-6
1968
TUES. THRU SUN.

they'd barbecue it and serve it in sandwiches on Saturday. The Wild West show eventually gave way to the rodeos that have long been a staple of fairs in the West and Midwest. Tingley Coliseum, built in 1957 at the New Mexico fairground specifically for indoor rodeo events, was christened by Roy Rogers and Dale Evans, and is now the site of the largest fair rodeo in the United States.

During the 1950s, stars from Hollywood and television began drawing huge crowds to their performances at fairs across the country. At the 1956 Ohio fair, for example, Hopalong Cassidy, Lassie, and Roy Rogers and Dale Evans appeared before the grandstand crowds; the next year, Ricky Nelson, Rin-Tin-Tin, and Tennessee Ernie Ford did shows.

Some fairgoers wanted to do more than spectate. For their amusement, fairs offered up a host of games and contests. Some of the classics are familiar to everyone, such as the Hi-Strike, where young men showed their strength by hitting a lever with a large mallet, trying to propel a weight up a wire to ring a bell at the top, and maybe win a cigar or some other prize in the process.

The C. W. Parker Amusement Company of Abilene, Kansas (later, in 1911, of Leavenworth), made mechanical shooting galleries and ball-throwing booths. During the 1870s and 1880s, the painted canvas targets included Mrs. O'Leary (whose cow burned Chicago); caricatures of blacks, Jews, and Irishmen; soldiers, police, and baseball catchers. Some targets were rigged so that a bullseye caused the target figure to fall into a tub of water. Some of the shooting gallery backdrops were as much as 20 feet wide, depicting forests, mountain scenery, Indian encampments, or a river bearing ducks and canoes. On

some layouts, Parker depicted girls who, when the shooter hit the target, had their clothing lifted to reveal their underwear. In another design, hitting the target caused a dog to tug a robe from a reclining girl.

If the Arkansas fair had coonskin caps as midway prizes this year, the carnies could have cleaned up even more effectively than usual.
Arkansas State Fair

Midway prizes offer nostalgic insight into the fads of the day. Six-inch dolls based on illustrator Rose O'Neill's Kewpies (which first appeared in her drawings for a children's story in the *Ladies' Home Journal* in 1909) had a few seasons as the hottest prize on the midway. In the early 1930s, the most popular prizes were Lindbergh dolls, boxes of candy, and Amos and Andy dolls. Shirley Temple dolls were the top choice in 1935.

Games and contests at fairs ranged from impromptu silliness to highly publicized, extremely competitive events that drew contestants from nearby states. As early as 1888, a fair in Rhode Island advertised bicycle races, polo games, steeple chasing, and various participatory contests involving greased poles, sacks, and wheelbarrows. Fairs often had bingo, sometimes called the "corn game" because players used kernels of corn.

**California fairgoers, represented by the mascot bear family at lower right, lined up to see entertainers Jack Benny and Xavier Cugat in 1952.** California State Fair

Xavier Cugat

Official PICTORIAL GUIDE BOOK

CALIFORNIA REPUBLIC

Jack Benny

CALIFORNIA STATE-FAIR NIGHT SHOW

CALIFORNIA STATE AGRICULTURAL SOCIETY

Price 50¢

CALIFORNIA STATE FAIR

SACRAMENTO · 1952 ·

"A good deal of human riffraff inevitably follows in the train of circuses, carnivals and fairs. And the visitors themselves constitute a motley crowd . . . many easily succumb to the lure of 'trying their luck,' testing their strength, treating themselves to the 'educational opportunities' offered by two-headed calves, pig-faced boys and Egyptian mummies, or indulging in various intemperances of eating, drinking and spending."

—WAYNE CALDWELL NEELY, *THE AGRICULTURAL FAIR*, 1968.

This classic midway contest, sometimes called the Hi-Strike, was a favorite of pickpockets, because spectators made easy marks as they craned their necks to watch the gong at the top. This example was at the Vermont State Fair in 1941. Jack Delano/Library of Congress, LC-USF35-36

The "Mouse Game" featured a circular board with 50 holes around the outer edge; folks bet which hole a mouse would run down. People competed to see who could sound most like a rooster. The winner of a hog-calling contest in 1959 produced, according to one account, a noise that sounded like "a sawmill, steam threshing machine and a love-struck cougar." The champion from the previous year told a reporter that he didn't think any particular style was best—whatever hogs got used to worked fine. Hog-calling contests have recently been supplemented with spouse-calling competitions. In 1946, the Nevada State Fair had a beard-growing contest, with prizes for the longest and the best-trimmed.

Cow-chip-tossing contests are a comparatively modern invention that quickly became a popular, attention-getting event at fairs. They seemed easy enough to arrange; expensive equipment wasn't required. When the Hawaii State Fair decided to offer this event one year, however, they had to import cow chips from Oklahoma.

Fairs have held archery matches, trapshooting tournaments (sometimes with several hundred shooters taking part), and fiddling contests (at the Ohio State Fair in 1925, this event drew 105 entrants, and this contest remains popular today). Horseshoe tournaments have long been serious business at state fairs ranging from New Jersey (which held state tournaments in the 1930s) to Ohio (where tournaments for farmers have been a daily activity at the fair for 50 years). In 1921 the Minnesota State Fair held a national horseshoe tournament that drew 300 players of both sexes. A contemporary photo showed the women's champion, tossing a shoe while togged out in a black dress, heels, stockings, and a stylish hat. The photo looked posed, but given the formality of the times, that may have been how women dressed to compete.

Tucked into a corner of the Pioneer Hall barn at the Iowa fairground is the National Horseshoe Pitchers Hall of Fame, where a blow-up of a 1924 newspaper article reveals that an estimated one million people had joined horseshoe clubs that year. The article was written by Theodore Allen, a national champion, and mentioned his record of 56 ringers in a row, and of 92 ringers out of 100. Clearly, the game had come a long way from the original version played with real horseshoes flung at a buggy axle stuck in the ground.

Hard-fought contests riveted spectators. At a California fair one year, Admiral Chester Nimitz became so engrossed in the championship that he missed an appointment to get his photo taken at an exhibit of Navy radar equipment.

The penny toss is a perfect midway game: it is cheap, requires little skill, is deceptively hard, and is still fun. The large prizes hanging overhead were called "flash," because they attracted attention. The biggest prizes are always far more difficult to win. This game was photographed in 1965. Florida State Fair

The winner raises his hand after a pie-eating contest at a 4-H club fair in Cimarron, Kansas, August 1939. Novelty contests at fairs go back to colonial times.
Russell Lee/Library of Congress, LC-USF-12379-M1

**Miss Nebraska State Fair poses with a pair of junior motorcyclists at a Nebraska State Fair in the 1960s.** Nebraska State Fair

Fairs also featured a spectrum of races, which, like contests, include both the earnest and the foolish. Through the years, crowds have watched contestants riding or driving bicycles, speedboats, chuck wagons, and chariots. Animal racers have included armadillos, camels, ostriches (sometimes pulling little two-wheeled buggies), and pigs. Ostrich trainers say the birds are best steered by covering one of their eyes with a small broom, depending which direction the driver wants to go. These crowd-pleasing and ever-hungry animals have been known to spot a tasty-looking straw hat in the crowd and go after it.

A spectrum of vendors, hawking an a-to-z assortment of toys, novelties, and gadgets, set up their booths in any open spot. In the 1930s, tiny bamboo canes, miniature clown hats, and toy monkeys on sticks were popular. At the Oregon State Fair in 1954, pitchmen sold decks of trick cards, pin-up photos (called, with typical euphemism, "art studies"), hair restorer, Brazilian (i.e., fake) diamond rings, potato peelers, spot removers, ever-sharp knives, and cheap watches. Vendors worked an intricate, seasonal cycle of fairs, covering as many states as possible; in the words of one fair manager, "These peripatetic characters show up like robins before each fair opens."

With fairgoers buffeted by a welter of demands for their attention and their dimes, sideshow pitchmen (also called talkers, barkers, and grinders) often had to put on virtuoso performances of their own to get people into the seats. They used noisemakers to attract attention: sirens, lengths of railroad iron, bass drums, large steel triangles, even steel bars run up and down the rivets on old water heaters. Their spiels were sometimes as entertaining as whatever show awaited inside the canvas.

A writer for *Scribner's* magazine in 1903 described one barker, a small man who wore a frock-coat, a derby, and a white bow tie. He looked like a Sunday-school superintendent, the writer explained, and "took

**Magicians and palm-readers invariably drew crowds—and the unwanted attention of fair managers who sought to ban them from the fairground. A local newspaper article about the 1921 Minnesota State Fair was entitled "Fortune Tellers' Activities at Fair Bring Complaints." The author noted that clairvoyants and palmists were "violating state law" that year. This photo was taken in the early 1900s at the Minnesota State Fair.** Minnesota Historical Society

**This sideshow talker, dressed in a safari outfit, summoned people to see giant snakes and other wondrous creatures.** Library of Congress, LC-USF35-52

"Silky, persuasive, sarcastic, deeply misleading, confidential, ingratiating, hugely adaptable, often insulting, and, at the core, impossible to ruffle by anything attributable to God, man, or nature."
—DESCRIPTION OF NATE EAGLE, "THE LAST OF THE GREAT CARNIVAL 'TALKERS,'" NEW YORKER, 1958.

me into his confidence," saying "it was high time I left the old farm and saw the world." At hand was a detailed, intimate view of the historic city of Cairo. "He was so kind and confidential about it that I felt really disappointed when I paid my dime and found in his tent a camel, a donkey, and a few Chicago Arabs," the writer observed.

By the 1950s, barkers had become "talkers," using microphones and loudspeakers, instead of the old megaphones. When the Minnesota fair offered three sideshows (a freak show, "Harlem in Havana," and "Moulin Rouge") on the midway, a corresponding trio of talkers worked the crowd as they made their circuit. Kenneth "Duke" Wilson of Venice, Florida, labeled "king of the talkers" in a contemporary article, was last; the best talker handled the third show because he had the last chance at the crowd's money. As always, psychology was at work. Ticket sellers did their jobs very slowly during the first few sales to make the crowd pile up, which in turn made the people in the back more anxious to get in. Talkers

repeated, "Show time! Show time!" over and over, even when the show was 45 minutes away.

Veteran barker Nate Eagle was profiled in a series of articles in the *New Yorker* in 1958, which described him as "the last of the great carnival 'talkers'." Author Robert L. Taylor described Eagle as "silky, persuasive, sarcastic, deeply misleading, confidential, ingratiating, hugely adaptable, often insulting, and, at the core, impossible to ruffle by anything attributable to God, man, or nature." For Eagle, exaggeration was an art form. Once, for a jungle tableau, he rented some chimpanzees and advertised them as gorillas. If anyone complained, he explained they were pygmy gorillas, very rare.

Two kinds of performers—freaks and cooch dancers—didn't have to depend on the verbal pyrotechnics of a talker, because they seemed to effortlessly attract audiences. The posters and spiels were exaggerated: the fat lady was never quite as colossal, and the skimpily clad dancers were never quite as bare. But audiences didn't hesitate to see for themselves.

"Now I let him work for free, because he and his spry little monkeys delight small fry and oldsters alike. Organ grinders are becoming as scarce as buggy whips."
—SANTA CLARA (CALIFORNIA) COUNTY FAIR MANAGER RUSSELL PETTIT, SATURDAY EVENING POST, 1950s.

# CHAPTER SEVEN

# Riding the Moon Rocket, the Octopus and the Spitfire

aces and stunt driving provided only vicarious pleasure, save for the few lucky, or reckless, entrants. Fairgoers would not get an exciting ride of their own until the turn of the 20th century, when the mighty Ferris wheel revolutionized the midway, sending it upward with giant metal and wood structures, whirling, spinning, chugging and churning to carry the brave and the curious over loops and arcs. The rollercoaster would follow, as would other rides, charting a course of increased size, power, and adrenaline that continues to this day.

The process had begun innocuously enough with the simple merry-go-round, whose place of honor among carnival rides is undisputed: carnies used to refer to it as "the First Ride." In a memoir of his 80 years working at the Indiana State Fair, employee Art Rice recalled that a merry-go-round and a Ferris wheel were the only rides in 1901, before the fair had a midway. A half-century later, when the Alaska State Fair got its first carnival rides in 1950, a carousel and a Ferris wheel were the first on the scene.

Although most rides appeared in crude, simple versions, the first Ferris wheel was the greatest one ever built. An engineer named George Washington Gale Ferris presented his awesome creation at the 1893 World's Columbian Exposition in Chicago. The Pittsburgh bridge-builder's behemoth towered 265 feet over the fairgrounds, its 125-foot wheel turning on a 56-ton axle that was the largest piece of steel ever forged. Thirty-six glass-enclosed gondolas, the size of streetcars, made leisurely, 10-minute revolutions and carried more than 1,750,000 riders during the course of the fair.

"When your child is on a merry-go-round, never, never, never wave to him as he passes you. Doing so will break into a golden moment, a blissful excursion on a prancing horse, into the land where dreams come true."

—CARNIVAL RULE OF BEHAVIOR, *SCRIBNER'S* MAGAZINE, AUGUST 1903

The wheel was dismantled, erected at the St. Louis Exposition in 1904, then taken down for good. Some of its steel was reforged into part of the USS *Illinois*, which steamed into battle during World War I. Other sections were used in building Dunn's Bridge across the Kankakee River in Indiana, 45 miles south of Chicago.

Builders of later generation wheels never matched the original in size, but attracted attention by producing double and triple wheels that lorded over fairgrounds across the nation. The Minnesota State Fair in 1941 featured a quadruple Ferris wheel, along with other mechanical attractions such as the Ridee-O, Octopus, Rocket, and Hey Day, which were whirling and spinning their excited riders in ways that George Ferris wouldn't have imagined.

Heights bother some people, so Ferris wheels aren't for everybody. But is there anyone who hasn't ridden a merry-go-round? When author Minnie Lee McGehee gathered recollections for her book about the Fluvanna, Virginia, fairs of the 1920s, her research was unanimous: "Of the midway, the carousel has been best remembered with the most nostalgia, perhaps because it is a symbol of childhood pleasures." Certainly it has always suited young and old alike.

**Nearly a century after its invention, the Ferris wheel remains a popular necessity at any self-respecting fairground.** State Fair of Oklahoma

**A West Virginia State Fair promotional poster.**
Eamswood Communications, Inc., for the State Fair of West Virginia

Early American carousels were modeled after British steam-driven carousels. These wonderful devices had seats shaped like sailing ships, balloons, and gondolas, as well as eagles, centaurs, ostriches, lions, camels, wolves, goats, roosters, donkeys, and cows. Ever innovative, in 1906 seats shaped like motor cars appeared. Some of these steam carousels were exported to Coney Island in the 1870s, offering people rides on a hand-painted, wooden menagerie: deer, kangaroos, tigers, giraffes, hippos, pigs, and chickens joined the stable of mounts.

After sundown, these carousels were dimly lit by a half-dozen kerosene lamps. Before long, they were studded with tiny electric lights, and mechanics had figured out a way to make the animals bob up and down as they made their gentle circuit. Technically called "overhead-crank galloping action" but sometimes referred to as the "jumping horse merry-go-round," this innovation was introduced at the turn of the century and was immediately popular. Some carousels had as much as 3 feet of up-and-down action.

Amusement park carousels were larger and more elaborate than mobile versions, since they didn't have to travel around. They had three, four, even five mounts abreast, with the fanciest ones on the outside where they were most visible; some models had two or three tiers. A large one might have nearly 100 mounts, perhaps a pair

**A double Ferris wheel beckons at the Vermont State Fair in 1941.** Jack Delano/Library of Congress, LC-USF35-53

This behemoth was the original Ferris wheel, introduced to a spellbound audience at the World's Columbian Exposition in Chicago in 1893. For 50¢, riders made two slow circuits, climbing to a peak of 261 feet.

Library of Congress, LC-USZ62-50927

"...along the way, vendors sold ice cream and caramel apples and a man with a sewing machine would put your name on a little felt Robin Hood hat for only a quarter."

—BOB SCROGGS, SEATTLE, WASHINGTON, RECALLING THE MISSOURI STATE FAIR OF 1929.

"When we got tired, we went back to Uncle Gus's concession stand and rested in the box of cushions that were rented to grandstand patrons. After the shows were well underway, he would take us up to the stands. Many of the things we saw on that stage later turned up on *The Ed Sullivan Show*. We ended the day by falling asleep in the cushion box until Uncle Gus was done and ready to take us home, two tired little girls."
— JOYCE WHORLEY, CORNELIUS, OREGON, RECALLING THE IONIA FREE FAIR OF THE 1930S AND 1940S.

**The Midway at night was one of the finest sights of the fair.** J. C. Allen and Son, Inc.

of Roman chariots, and a couple of small, round, enclosed, revolving seats called "lovers' tubs."

In the early 1900s, the horse began taking over as the mount of choice. Some carousels, such as the one at the Illinois State Fair in 1907, featured a "king horse," which was larger and fancier than the other mounts, offering the rider a chance to grab a brass ring suspended from a rail overhead. The Illinois carousel stood in Happy Hollow, the central site for the sideshows and rides that had once been scattered around the fairgrounds.

The popularity of carousels is attested to by a letter in the Arizona State Fair archives. The document is dated October 1909 and addressed to the Merry-Go-Round Company of Quincy, Illinois. A Phoenix judge wanted to buy or rent a carousel so that his son could operate it as a concession at the fair. "I have never heard of any of the merry-go-rounds of yours here or in the Territory," he wrote. The archives don't reveal if he received one.

The horses on carousels gradually became more elaborate; they appeared to be tossing their heads, their manes ruffled by an imaginary wind. Elaborately carved secondary figures (eagles, serpents, lion's heads) decorated saddles and flanks; one depicted Teddy Roosevelt in his Rough Riders uniform along with a tiger. Seats from the 1920s included storks, zebras, frogs, and dogs. The C. W. Parker Amusement Company of Kansas created huge, extravagant horses that expressed speed and motion in an extraordinary way.

The Minnesota State Fair gave riders an exciting new opportunity in 1920. That year it installed two new rides. One was a merry-go-round, and the other was its opposite: the stomach-churning, scream-producing rollercoaster.

The coaster in America also owes its genesis to Coney Island, where, in 1884, fun-seekers rode America's first "amusement railway." Small coasters had appeared in Paris as early as 1804; the first looping coaster in France was demonstrated in 1848, but these early designs were essentially large sleds that ran over rollers, which put severe technical limitations on the ride's potential. But at Coney Island, when La Marcus Thompson opened his 450-foot Switchback Gravity Pleasure Railway in June 1884, the future of the rollercoaster suddenly opened into a white-knuckled expanse. Thompson's cars held 10 people and rolled down gently undulating inclines, reaching a thrilling speed of six miles per hour. At a nickel a ride, Thompson earned back his investment in three weeks.

Soon the race was on to continually improve on this success. Thompson added a tunnel with the new electric lights that came on when the train hit a switch. Other park operators added tunnels and scenery, creating rides with names such as "Pikes Peak" and "The Alps." But because many fairgoers preferred terror to scenery, adrenaline production rapidly became a central theme in rollercoaster design. In 1888 America's first looping coaster, the Flip-Flap, appeared at Coney Island. The 10-second ride produced a neck-wrenching 12 Gs of force on riders. The Flip-Flap looked so dangerous that folks paid a dime just to watch others ride it.

Although the danger of rollercoasters was largely illusory, early designs were far from foolproof. In 1910,

This undated poster for the State Fair of West Virginia shows a Ferris wheel that appears to lack restraining bars, along with a carousel, swings, and a ride that appears to be a Whip (left rear). Eamswood Communications, Inc., for the State Fair of West Virginia

"In 1904, when I was six years old, my grandmother and I traveled from Sedalia to St. Louis for the sole purpose of seeing all the wonderful displays at the state fair. We rode on the first Ferris wheel. I don't know how long it took me to coax Granny to ride on 'that contraption,' but I did. The seating spaces looked like chicken coops, because there was wire fencing on all sides. The seats were two long benches, back to back, in the center. I enjoyed the ride a lot, and Granny did, too, after she saw that strong wire all around, we couldn't possibly fall out."
—FRANCES ROETTGERS, BRIGHTON, ILLINOIS.

A small Ferris wheel anchored the North Georgia Fair in Barrow County, Georgia, in 1918. The fair was discontinued in the late 1920s. Georgia Department of Archives and History

On a warm summer night in 1963, two young speedsters work hard to negotiate a tough turn in their race car.
Iowa State Fair, Des Moines

A Round-Up at the 1967 Oklahoma State Fair. State Fair of Oklahoma

Even the smallest of rides could provide big thrills for the children at the 1940 Delta County Fair in Colorado. Russell Lee/Library of Congress, LC-USF35-257

on a Coney Island coaster called the Rough Riders (which featured a steep downgrade with a sharp curve at the bottom), two cars tore loose and sailed over the edge of the scaffold, 60 feet above Surf Avenue. Of the 16 people who fell, 4 died.

In spite of such occasional mayhem, a craze for rollercoasters swept the nation. The Indiana State Fair of 1916 boasted a 2,000-foot, "high speed" rollercoaster as a new attraction. Histories of the Iowa State Fair refer to that fair's rollercoaster as "new" in 1915. The coaster fell into disrepair during World War II; it hadn't been kept painted, and much of it had rotted.

A seminal coaster design, the Cyclone, appeared in 1927 at Coney Island. Its 83-foot incline brought cars to 55 miles per hour, with a sharp curve at the bottom. The ride lasted 1 minute and 40 seconds. Orville Wright and Charles Lindbergh gave it rave reviews. The coaster was built with a noticeable amount of give in its wooden trusses; this flex gave it a rickety feeling, but actually helped the structure handle the stresses produced by the heavy cars.

Those who wanted to laugh rather than scream were delighted by a walk-through (or, more accurately, stumble-through) attraction that gradually became known as the Fun House. Carnivals later included mobile versions,

using some of the innovations of an entrepreneur and theater operator named George C. Tilyou, whose Steeplechase Park at Coney Island was one of America's first amusement parks. Tilyou invented the Funny Stairway with its comical collapsing steps, and the Barrel of Fun, whose revolutions invariably sent the folks inside sprawling as they tried to walk through.

Writing in 1909, Rollin Hartt described this peculiar-but-beloved attraction, which he referred to as "the Foolish House": "The floor wallows and shakes. Horrifying bumps confront your feet. What with tempest and

**Do-it-yourself fun at the 1933 Indiana State Fair. Nowadays, people would call this "exercise" rather than entertainment.** J. C. Allen and Son, Inc.

**Four generations ago, Minnesota's John Keenan built what is now the Minnesota State Fair's oldest ride (and the Iowa State Fair's oldest ride, as well): the tunnel of love called Ye Olde Mill. Now, the third generation of the Keenan family (John H. Keenan, Sr., in the red shirt) and the fourth generation (Jim, Joe, Jer, and John, Jr., in the blue shirts) keep the popular old ride running. The ride's yellow paddlewheel is visible in the rear.** Ye Olde Mill Amusements, Inc.

A small rollercoaster at the Florida State Fair in 1957. This scene was at the old fairground in the heart of Tampa. Florida State Fair

earthquakes and night and labyrinthine confusion and stumbling blocks combined, you wish yourself dead. Then relief! A crystal maze, humorous but alarming. A row of concave and convex mirrors, showing you yourself as Humpty Dumpty." This sight produced, Hartt said, five minutes of laughter.

Another ride, the tunnel of love, more often produced five minutes of heavy breathing. The Iowa and Minnesota fairs retain historic examples of this classic ride called the Old Mill (or Ye Olde Mill). The pairs of rides are all that remain of seven originally built by John H. Keenan of Minnesota at fairgrounds in the Midwest between 1912 and 1915. Keenan had begun his career managing vaudeville theaters in Philadelphia and had transitioned into amusement rides with the demise of that genre. The Iowa version has been in continuous use since 1912. Originally a dark, enclosed, 950-foot canal made of tarred wood, it was rebuilt in 1996, following the original specifications. A large red paddlewheel is the only original part left. The Minnesota ride, built a year later, is still in its original building. Keenan's grandson, who shares the

The Loop-O-Plane was one of the very first midway rides that inverted passengers, and the crowds loved the sensation. This ride was at the 1936 Indiana State Fair. J. C. Allen and Son, Inc.

same name, now manages the historic ride, which is the oldest existing tunnel of love in the United States.

In June 1935, *Popular Mechanics* ran an article entitled "Mechanical Fun-Makers Add New Thrills to Modern Carnivals," by Edwin Teale. His survey offers a whirlwind ride down the memory lane of amusement machinery. He described a dozen rides that fairgoers could anticipate for the coming season. Teale led off with a pair of what he called "new nerve-tinglers": the Loop-the-Loop and the Loop-O-Plane. On the former, groups of four people rode in drum-shaped cages. On the Loop-O-Plane, riders sat in streamlined cars that were attached to long, metal arms.

Another ride was already a classic midway attraction: the Whip, named after the playground game of crack the whip. Small, metal, tub-shaped cars, attached to a central pole by metal arms and powerful springs, yanked riders around a flat, elliptical metal surface. At the end of each swing, the car accelerated around the corner with a burst of speed. The W. F. Mangels Co. had marketed the ride nationwide in 1914. Previous devices had jogged riders up and down, or revolved them in large circles, but all were sedate. The Whip had everyone grabbing for support.

"The old-fashioned Whip has been replaced by the Hey Day and the Caterpillar."
—TRENDS IN MIDWAY RIDES, 1947.

The Whip, invented 18 years before this photo was made in 1932, was immediately popular because of the burst of acceleration produced by the curve at each end of the track. J. C. Allen and Son, Inc.

At Georgia's Winder Fair, circa 1960, the Round-Up cost a mere dime. Versions of this ride are still common at carnivals and fair midways. Ideally, the riders' lunches continued to obey gravity during the furious spinning, even if the ride defied it.
Georgia Department of Archives and History

It proved a popular and durable attraction for generations, until a 1947 article pointed out, "The old-fashioned Whip has been replaced by the Hey Day and the Caterpillar," two newer rides mentioned by Teale. The Spillman Engineering Company had begun producing the Caterpillar in 1922; one history of carnival rides described it as "a money maker on all shows that could get delivery of one." The Caterpillar was a continuous train on a small, circular track that rose and fell a few feet. When the ride started, the cars were open; during the ride, a canvas top slid over and enclosed the riders; amorous couples could then smooch away, tunnel-of-love-style, until the top slid back. Waiting riders whooped and hollered at couples caught in the clinch.

Some of the 1935 rides had staying power: the Ridee-O, one of the fastest rides built before the war, was clanking away on the midway at the 1951 Nebraska State Fair. It first appeared in the late 1920s, and featured cars that traveled in circles on metal arms, rising and falling as they revolved.

The 68 hand-carved wooden horses from this carousel, a memorable feature of the Minnesota State Fair for three-quarters of a century, were saved from the auction block by a community effort in 1988. It was originally built in 1914 by the Philadelphia Toboggan Company.
Our Fair Carousel, photo by Joel Sheagren

This pinto pony with a leopard-skin saddle shows the fine detail and energetic carving of the old handmade carousel mounts. Formerly at the Minnesota state fairground, it continues to charm riders both young and old at a local park.

An assortment of whirling, speeding, and turning rides offered Vermont fairgoers thrills ranging from mild to extreme—or what passed for extreme in the prewar days. The ride at left was often called a Waltzer. Jack Delano/Library of Congress, LC-USF35-39

Teale didn't describe all of the rides he mentioned, and because their names weren't standardized, some designs remain a mystery. Does anyone remember the Leaping Lena? Or a late-1940s ride called the Rocket, described in an article in the *Christian Science Monitor* as "an atomic bomb with its tail in its mouth, which dashes wildly along a circular track"?

Fair managers used new rides as promotional gimmicks. The New Jersey State Fair in 1936, featuring a midway provided by William Glick Exposition Shows, advertised that it contained "every new riding device made in the past five years."

Every season, state fairs bragged about the extent of their mechanical arsenal. The 1941 Minnesota fair had more than two dozen, including the Spitfire. Mounted on a platform with a 45-degree slope, the ride's cars were shaped like aircraft with wings and controls that let riders "fly" them like airplanes. The 1951 Nebraska State Fair presented a collection of 21 that advertisements called "modern and thrilling riding devices," including the Moon Rocket, Rollo-plane, Auto Scooters, Ghost Ride, Jet Planes, Kiddie Autos, Merry-Mixup, Crazy Castle (no doubt a modernized, portable version of Tilyou's Fun House), and the Wall of Death. The 1953

This small carousel offered rides on miniature vehicles instead of the usual horses at the South Louisiana State Fair in Donaldsonville, November 1938. Russell Lee/Library of Congress, LC-USF33-11780-M3

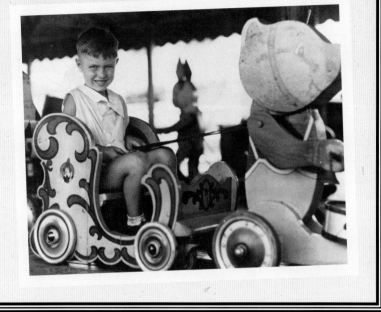

"Of the midway, the carousel has been best remembered with the most nostalgia, perhaps because it is a symbol of childhood pleasures."
—MINNIE LEE MCGEHEE, WRITING ABOUT THE FLUVANNA, VIRGINIA, FAIRS OF THE 1920S.

It wasn't every day that you got to harness up a bear drummer. This happy rider was piling up the memories at the 1934 Minnesota State Fair. Kenneth Wright, Minnesota Historical Society

Army recruiters sponsored this attraction for kids. Who knows how many future members of Army Airborne got their start this way? State Fair of Oklahoma

Minnesota fair boasted six Ferris wheels and "the sensational new Hurricane."

In spite of the continuous innovations of the speed rides, the humble carousel kept its constant and popular place. Perhaps unfortunately, the old hand-carved wooden mounts skyrocketed in value as art objects. Some were worth as much as $50,000. In 1988 the owners of the carousel at the Minnesota fairground decided to cash in. The 68 ponies, all carved in 1914 by the Philadelphia Toboggan Company, were destined to be auctioned individually in New York City. Since they had been used at the fair for only 6 to 12 days per year, they were in excellent shape. To retain this piece of midway heritage, a St. Paul nonprofit group called Our Fair Carousel took out a loan for $1.1 million and installed the historic ride in a local mall, where about 20,000 people per month rode it. It has since moved to Como Park, a huge recreation area just a few blocks from its old home at the fairground.

Some people were surprised that an old carousel would be worth a million dollars, but to the children who had ridden it during the previous 80 years, it had always been priceless.

"An atomic bomb with its tail in its mouth, which dashes wildly along a circular track . . ."
—CHRISTIAN SCIENCE MONITOR DESCRIBING A LATE-1940S RIDE CALLED THE ROCKET.

# CHAPTER EIGHT

# Something You Don't See at Home

In 1901, a fair in Anderson, South Carolina, advertised a pair of sideshow celebrities: Jo-Jo the Dog-Faced Boy and Little Egypt. Whether these two characters were the genuine article is doubtful (sideshow operators often traded on famous names with local substitutes). But what is interesting about the South Carolina fair's slate of attractions is how it linked the physically grotesque and the physically attractive. For some reason—some strange polarity of attraction—fairgoers were equally drawn to the beauty and the beast.

Jo-Jo was well-known as a "human oddity"; Little Egypt became the best known of the exotic dancers who burst on the American entertainment scene at the World's Columbian Exposition in Chicago in 1893. At the huge Chicago fair, the main draw was the North African dancing girls in the Algerian and Egyptian theaters, performing the *danse du ventre* (literally "dance of the belly"). The attraction called Cairo Street featured dozens of shops, shows, and a replica of a mosque, but the crowds didn't come to ride the camels and donkeys. They wanted to see the dancers.

Men thronged in, often followed by their wives, intently monitoring what their husbands were so interested in. It didn't matter that the show was less salacious than visitors assumed. Dancers wore baggy trousers, or multiple petticoats, bloomers and stockings, and loose, midriff-length tops; the dance involved an energetic series of spins, shoulder and hip shimmies, hip locks, and pirouettes. Incredibly tame by the standards of even 20 years later, performances were nevertheless packed for the duration of the fair.

"When I was a boy, my father told me I shouldn't go to the cooch show. Of course I asked, 'Why not?' and he said it was because I might see something I shouldn't see. Well, I went, and he was right. I saw my father."

—OLD BURLESQUE JOKE

Little Egypt's name rapidly became legend. Writing in *Scribner's* magazine in 1903, an anonymous author recounted the spiel at a country fair for a dancer who went by that name: "She has danced before the crowned heads of Europe," the barker announced. "She has been petted an' dined by the aylite of the world's capitals, an' is on her way to appear in the opery-house in New York." But the writer was skeptical; every fair seemed to have the same celebrated dancer (she was, in fact, appearing then at Coney Island). He called her "Little Egypt, the omnipresent!" Every large carnival carried a "Streets of Cairo" show until the early 1910s.

Little Egypt and her myriad sisters had emerged, with spectacular results, from a long but little-documented tradition of fair attractions that featured exotic beauties. Tantalizing evidence appears in the Michigan State Board of Agriculture's biennial report for 1880–1882, which described one of the so-called "hazards" of the Michigan State Fair: "An honest granger, desirous of visiting Art Hall—mistakes the entrance, and plunges unceremoniously into a bear den; or, into the dangerous midst of a band of painted, bloodthirsty scalping savages. Seeking to escape, he rushes suddenly into the awful presence of the 'Circassian Beauty,' that captivating syren, who has

Cowboy Jack Hoxie (on the machine at left) lost out to the attractions of the Wiggling Wonders at this peep show at the Imperial County (California) Fair in March 1942. Russell Lee/Library of Congress, LC-USF34-72233-D

infested agricultural fairs, ever since the birth of the oldest inhabitant" (an old meaning of "awful" was "highly impressive"). If the oldest inhabitant was 80, sideshow "syrens" had appeared as early as 1800, a time when fairs included such antique attractions as gouging matches, grinning contests, and greased-pole climbs.

This particular siren may not have been Circassian, an ancient people from European Russia. Long noted for their beauty, they were tall, with oval faces, brown eyes, and rich, chestnut hair. And whether the Michigan farmer preferred a pretty painting to a pretty woman is open to considerable debate. For the public record, at least, respectable folks had to pretend that "captivating syrens" were scandalous.

But public attitudes toward sexuality were changing. As author David Nasaw observed in *Going Out: The Rise and Fall of Public Amusements*, ogling the gyrations of belly dancers was acceptable because they were performing "authentic" foreign dances, culturally enriching citizens who couldn't travel overseas. In much the same way, a pretty young woman wearing tights or a snug bathing suit could appear on stage in the role of acrobat or championship swimmer, which excused a revealing costume that would otherwise be inappropriate.

Exotic dancers soon were mandatory at these events, becoming generically known as Fatimas. A sample spiel from 1909 proclaimed that one particular Fatima was a Bedouin from Nineveh, and that she performed the "mystic anaconda dance, exactly as danced by Hypatia in Holy Writ." This melange of foreign names sounded authentic to an uneducated audience, although it was a hopeless hodgepodge of history. Bedouins are a nomadic Arab tribe from Arabia, Syria, and North Africa; Nineveh was in Assyria, now part of Iraq. Anacondas slither through the jungles of South America. But fairgoers were interested in anatomy, not history or geography.

The romantic-sounding foreign names often belied the reality. An article in *Colliers* in 1913 described the women beneath the hype: "La Belle Fatima, a disgusting, dour, red-faced old woman; Oskalina, a slender girl who had to keep fidgeting in order to live up to the barker's explanation that her muscles could no longer keep still; and Algeria, a tall, light-haired girl who looked as if she might have been cashier in a dairy restaurant."

Until about 1920, cooch (a word derived from "hoochie-coochie") girls sometimes worked as hostesses and dancing partners in a type of show called the "'49 Camp," a simulated dance hall from the days of the California Gold Rush. These attractions became notorious for pushing the lines of propriety, and resulted in many towns banning carnivals.

Urban burlesque quickly became what Morton Minsky, whose family ran New York's best-known burlesque theaters in the 1920s, described as "a legal way of selling the illusion of sex to the public." The trend inspired hundreds of cooch dancers to seek new audiences in the small towns and villages that traveling carnivals visited during agricultural fairs.

At amusement parks, a certain amount of harmless, faintly sexual play crept into the midway experience. Fun houses sometimes had air nozzles concealed in the floor; when the operator flipped a switch, a blast of air raised women's long, bulky skirts. Amusement-park genius George Tilyou invented this innocent gag for his Blowhole Theater at Steeplechase Park on Coney Island. The path to ribald and on to raunchy was direct and tempting. On the midway, racy dances readily became strip shows, generally mild at large state fairs (where dancers usually wore their g-strings until the finale).

**The exhibit in the background promises a view of "The World at War," but this crowd is interested in an even more primal attraction: pretty girls. This scene was photographed at the Minnesota State Fair in 1917.** Minnesota Historical Society

Doc Cunningham, a longtime employee of the Iowa State Fair who recalls the girlie shows of the 1940s, says that even at the end of the shows, the girls were still wearing the equivalent of a bikini. After a few visits, he discovered that the pitch for the show was deceptive. The girls would come out on the bally as a sort of preview, he explains. "They were all pretty good looking and pretty well built," and they led you to believe that hot stuff awaited during the real show. "You thought it would be better inside, but it wasn't," he says. A typical incident in the mid-1930s centered around dancer Jade Rhedora. Rumors circulated on the fairground that she was dancing stark naked. A state legislator named Gus Alesch investigated; the pitchman outside indeed promised complete nudity, and Alesch confirmed it when he went inside. "Not so much as a piece of corn plaster interposed itself between the goggle-eyed public and the girls' epidermis," he declared. But it turned out his eyesight wasn't quite perfect in the dim tent, because Rhedora and her troupe were wearing flesh-colored tights.

The incident garnered national publicity, and the show made lots of money.

Fair promoter George Hamid quickly discovered that male audiences became hostile when they weren't offered an extra act called a "blow-off" after the regular exotic dance; blow-offs were private shows for men only, usually costing an extra quarter. Flimsy veils and diaphanous skirts were standard for the main show; shedding these costumes was the key to the blow-off.

Cooch shows were popular across the country. In the mid-1930s, *Time* magazine could declare, without fear of contradiction, that only one fairgoer out of 10 wanted to see the agricultural exhibits. The other nine preferred girls "undraped, unveiled and unashamed," along with auto racing, rodeo, and the midway. Describing the midway at the Iowa State Fair, another *Time* writer observed, "Nobody ever got trampled inspecting a colt in the Horse Barn. But last week many a toe got stepped on while its owner ogled a filly named Jade Rhedora," the stripper mentioned above.

> **"You thought it would be better inside, but it wasn't."**
> —DOC CUNNINGHAM, LONGTIME EMPLOYEE OF THE IOWA STATE FAIR, RECALLING GIRLIE SHOWS OF THE 1940S.

SHOW GIRLS OF THE CLUB LIDO POSE FOR A PUBLICITY PHOTO.

**These showgirls probably relied on fancy costumes, dramatic light and dancing instead of bare flesh to draw crowds. By the 1950s, most cooch shows at large state fairs did the same. At smaller, transient fairs, however, it was a different story.**
Minnesota State Fair

beautiful," author Phil Stong wrote in *Holiday* magazine in August 1948, "and Sally herself, only a lovely clean-cut face above the slowly moving ostrich plumes, is a new kind of State Fair enchantress."

Rand toured with Royal American Shows, a company that also brought Gypsy Rose Lee and Bonnie Baker to fairs at that time. The years from 1946 through 1954 were prime time for the big-name stars; Gypsy Rose Lee and Sally Rand were probably the highest-paid features any carnival ever carried—and they were worth it. Nevertheless, midways at large, established fairs were beginning to dispense with girlie shows, concentrating on rides and games. One reason, Doc Cunningham observes, was that women were beginning to wear clothes that were tight, skimpy, or revealing in public as part of their normal attire, and men could watch them all day long for free.

At smaller fairs and vagabond carnivals in remote areas, however, dancers could get away with more provocative displays, and cooch shows continued with unabated vigor. Into the 1950s, a few state fairs still offered shows that at least appeared to have lascivious themes. At the Michigan State Fair in 1950, the cooch show was called "Satan's Children." Warnings about the perils of white slavery served as an excuse for erotic displays. The ostensible rationale for the show (to warn impressionable young women, who hardly made up the usual strip-show audience) was as flimsy as the outfits of the performers.

In the early 1950s, the James Strates carnival (which provided midways for numerous state fairs) offered a sideshow called "The Harem," starring entertainer Chloe Carter, in which the girls danced for a large mannequin dressed like a sultan. The record doesn't reveal whether the show included an indictment of polygamy.

Although fairs were often segregated—particularly in the South prior to the Civil Rights movement—the

Large midways usually offered revues of dancing girls. Although they weren't particularly profitable, they were known as "committee shows" because they were appropriate for fair managers and their wives. During the 1930s, girl revues built into large productions, with 10-piece stage bands, as many as a dozen girls, vaudeville acts, and comedians.

Sally Rand, who drew crowds of 10,000 for her famous fan dancing at the 1947 Iowa fair, took her version of cooch in a wholesome direction. "The dance is

popularity of cooch crossed racial lines. The 1958 edition of the West Texas Fair had both black and white girlie shows, with equally raucous audiences, according to one account. "'Shake it, gal!' they yelled, happily ignorant that dancer Anita Lopez was a bewigged male," a contemporary magazine writer noted, attending a performance that was even more exotic than the audience realized.

What sort of girl became a cooch dancer? Most have long since vanished into obscurity, but one, a stripper named Francine Victoria Flanagan, left her impressions in an article published in the *New York Times* magazine in 1952. She was born in London Bridge, Virginia, the daughter of a flamenco dancer and a sailor. As a young woman, she once taught at a backwoods school where, she recalled, most of the students didn't wear shoes until November. She vastly preferred the carnie life, she told writer Gilbert Millstein. "You've seen me standing out on the bally, kibitzing with the customers. I love 'em. They're paying, aren't they?"

Strippers rarely had long careers, but Flanagan, for one, didn't intend to slip into obscurity. She had surprising plans for her life after cooch. She intended to become an evangelist, traveling with a fleet of purple trucks, carrying a supporting cast of reformed drunks, criminals, and thieves. She planned to dress as an angel, with a long white gown and mechanical wings that she could flutter. Alas, this virtuous scheme had a mundane motive. She knew that Billy Graham was charging a dollar or two per customer. She planned to up the ante.

The anti-cooch legions would have been overjoyed to learn they had a potential evangelist in the opposing camp. As was the case with freak shows, moralists and reformers had been trying to get rid of strippers for decades. In an editorial in a March 1903 issue of *Billboard*, Will S. Heck (general manager of the General Amusement Company of Cincinnati) described the itinerant carnivals that typically hosted strip shows as "a lot of vulgar, immoral, disgusting exhibitions aggregated under a collection of dirty, ragged canvas." This type of show, Heck declared, "leaves a stench that reaches from earth to sky, filling the nostrils of the law-abiding public."

For every Francine Flanagan who enjoyed driving the farm boys wild, there were grim tales of exploitation. A typical exposé from 1922 described cooch shows as a plague that had claimed and corrupted hundreds of farm girls, swallowing them up in an "unhealthy, degrading life."

> "The marks out there don't want a chorus line; they don't want show tunes; they don't want choreography or ballet. All they want is sex—bumps and grinds—they want to see something they don't see at home."
> —COOCH DANCER PAGAN JONES, LATE 1960s.

Cooch show promoters found all sorts of pseudo-moralistic excuses to exhibit scantily-clad girls. It is a safe bet that the audience at this "daring exposé" at a fair in Lancaster County, Pennsylvania, in May 1938, was more concerned with how much female flesh would be exposed.
Library of Congress

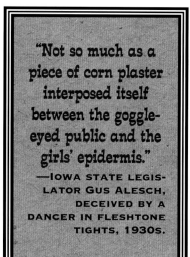

"They die of tuberculosis and pneumonia, among strangers; their unmarked graves are scattered up and down the land," the anonymous author wrote. This heart-rending diatribe, which sounds like the anti-marijuana film *Reefer Madness*, proved similarly ineffective. "Estelle in the Well" acts, in which men paid to gape at an almost naked girl lying at the bottom of a very shallow well and (for an extra 25 cents) could actually touch her, continued to be popular.

As with the aforementioned Jade Rhedora incident, accusations of scandalous shows—usually with little proof—were common. During the 1939 Indiana State Fair, for example, watchdogs of the Laymen's Civic Legion (a group of self-appointed protectors of morality) stirred up bad publicity with allegations of drinking, gambling, and lewd shows on the midway. State Senator E. Curtis White, a member of the fair board, said the reports were exaggerated. White admitted that there had been a lewd show a couple years earlier, but that it had been shut down right away. He said he had seen shows that were "10 times worse" at local theaters. Further defending the fair, Lieutenant Governor Henry Schricker said, "Now, we remember a time . . . days before Prohibition Days, when bootleggers were posted at every barn and on the grounds and were actually selling bootleg liquor. We gathered up whiskey bottles by the load when the Fair was over. . . ."

Some local attempts to censor midways were more direct and successful. New Hampshire's Deerfield Fair had a director in the 1940s whose wife was a reverend at a local church. One day she spied some cooch dancers rehearsing a strip show and promptly ordered her husband to get rid of them. He did, and cooch dancers never returned to that fair.

Deerfield was the exception, however. Girlie shows in traveling carnivals more than held their own through the 1950s and the 1960s, when the editor of a trade journal responded to a query about the most popular carnival attractions by putting girl shows at the top of his list. Fair managers might deny it, trying to present a wholesome image to the public, but cooch brought in the boys. Almost every carnival, especially the small ones, carried at least one girl show. Some traveling carnivals in the rural South had three or four different shows; customers often spent the night going from one to another.

Jade Rhedora went on the record affirming her enjoyment of performing at fairs. She wouldn't take off her clothes at nightclubs or stag parties, she told a magazine writer. Fair midways were different. "The people are really good folks," she said. "They don't get to see much of this sort of thing and they get a thrill out of it."

## A Cooch Girl's Tale

"Plenty of girls that are stars now were nothing but cooch dancers in road shows when they started. . . . That's the way I started myself. My girl friend and I, we were still in high school and one summer this carnival comes along. We were both kind of wild and crazy, we wanted to get away from home and see the world. We were sick of school and getting hell when we stayed out late at night, and we were sick of the silly boys around town. So we went out with these fellows from the carnival. We thought they were swell, the real McCoy. They dressed snappy and talked big city stuff, and we ate it up. . . . They had a couple of girls with the show, a couple of cooch dancers, and them girls got burned up because they fooled around with us. They had a big jamboree one night, a hell of a fight, and both girls quit the show and scrammed. So the guys put us in the show. God! But I was scared the first time I went on, and so was Kitty. We were both natural dancers—you don't have to do much dancing in a cooch tent anyway—but we were scared. "Of course there were men and boys who knew us and that made it worse. But we said to hell with them. It was our chance to get a start and we were going to take it, so we went out there and stripped down and shook it for them. The other girls showed us how to shake it good enough to get by. In that kind of a show all they want you to do is strip and squirm around. . . .

"We traveled all over the state with that bunch. . . . We thought it was a great life. All that money to spend on clothes and things; nobody to tell us what to do or when to go to bed, and all kinds of men after us. But the show broke up in the fall, and our two guys took a powder, beat it without a word. And the rats took our last week's pay besides. I guess that was our first real lesson."

—"STILL GOING PLACES," PUBLISHED IN *AMERICAN LIFE HISTORIES: MANUSCRIPTS FROM THE FEDERAL WRITERS PROJECT, 1936–1940,* SEPTEMBER 14, 1940.

Century 21 Shows
PRESENTS
BRODWAY

Pagan Jones, a cooch dancer during the late 1960s, agreed, announcing that she would much rather perform at fair midways than at urban nightclubs, where, she said, the customers just drank, smoked, and talked. Jones said these urban audiences were distracted and uncommunicative. The audiences at fairs and carnivals, though, were more direct and expressive. "The marks out there don't want a chorus line; they don't want show tunes; they don't want choreography or ballet," she explained. "All they want is sex—bumps and grinds—they want to see something they don't see at home."

Ah, something they didn't see at home . . . that was how it all started back with Little Egypt before the turn of the century. And lo and behold, at the Indiana State Fair in 1952, advertisements promised two girl shows: a troupe billed as the "Hi Steppers of 1952" and none other than Little Egypt. Since the real Little Egypt had died in 1937, this dancer was merely the latest incarnation of Little Egypt, the omnipresent. But she was no doubt curvaceous and perhaps promiscuous, and the audience didn't mind at all.

**Risqué banners circa 1967 do their best to distract fairgoers from the mechanical rides competing for attention. The big question, as always, was whether the actual show was as daring as the artwork.** Iowa State Fair, Des Moines

# CHAPTER NINE

# Missing Link Meets Alligator Boy

Guests at Vermont's Tunbridge Hotel during the famous Tunbridge World's Fair witnessed a strange scene each morning: two shrouded figures, one huge and one small, meeting in the lobby and leaving the hotel. Carrying open umbrellas draped with long, opaque curtains that hung to the ground, the outlandish pair headed toward the fair. There, they vanished behind the canvas tents lining the midway, where a garish banner revealed the mystery of their identity: blocky red letters spelled out the magic word "Freaks," above a painting of a woman the size of a haystack and a tiny man standing in a teacup.

Later, farmers and tourists packed the dim tent, as a leather-lunged barker on a wooden platform out front bellowed, "See the world's smallest man!" and "See the world's fattest lady!" amid a torrent of fancy adjectives and exhortations.

The umbrellas were a clever way to draw attention. And they were practical; every local resident who viewed the freaks for free meant one less dime in the midway till. Who could help but stare? At country fairs, almost everyone had seen Holsteins and Leghorns, but not everyone had seen a dog boy, a bird woman, a human pincushion, or a man who could stuff four golf balls in his mouth.

Such unusual or grotesque sights exert a powerful allure. To capitalize on this fact of human nature, from the Civil War through the 1950s, freak shows were par for the course at fair midways. At the 1937 Iowa State Fair, the spotlight fell on the Man with India-Rubber Skin and Percilla, the Monkey Girl. Nebraska's 1951 fair presented the Congress of Oddities, "with unbelievable freaks of nature on exhibit, from all parts of the world."

> "Almost always they are in their very nature degrading and often, disgusting. The whole sideshow atmosphere is one of deception, and there the fakir's art reaches its highest development."
>
> —ANNOUNCEMENT BY EIGHT STATE FAIR OFFICIALS

These strange people represented the dark side of the usually wholesome country fair. In this pen, you have a blue-ribbon hog; on that stage, the world's fattest human. Here, a beauty queen from a nearby town; there, a wild man from Borneo. The agricultural pavilion was packed with picture-perfect examples of cattle and sheep; on the midway lurked the deformed and the loathsome. These two discordant elements—the normal and abnormal, the mainstream and the shocking—had coexisted for so long at fairs that folks took them for granted.

As with other elements of American fairs, the phenomenon of the freak show dated back to the 18th century and wasn't a domestic invention. English colonists fondly remembered "van shows," named after the wooden carts that brought freaks, menageries, magicians, fortune tellers, and dancers from village to village during market fairs. An 1826 fair in Essex, England, for example, exhibited male and female giants, albinos, and a dwarf.

Mutant animals and human freaks were prime exhibits at popular museums (also known as "cabinets of curiosity") in America during the early 19th century, where they appeared along with scientific oddities and wax figures of famous and infamous characters. Scholars and snobs, who expected museums to be silent tombs hung with serious art, scorned this hodgepodge of attractions. In 1870 an

**"Hermaphrodite" Roberta Roberts headlined this freak show at the Indiana State Fair in 1934. Often, the shocking attributes were all in the makeup.** J. C. Allen and Son, Inc.

"As a young child in 1921, I went to the fair in Nashville with my mother and father. They let me go in a sideshow where the midgets were. I fell in love with them and forgot to come out. They were a married couple. Dressed so beautiful, they danced and entertained. My mother came in to get me. My father was real upset with me. I said, 'Oh, Papa, they are the cutest little people you ever saw.' I still love midgets."

—VERA PATTERSON, NASHVILLE, TENNESSEE.

The Midget Village at Chicago's Century of Progress exposition in 1933 was considered one of sideshow maestro Nate Eagle's crowning achievements.

English visitor sniffed, "a 'Museum' in the American sense of the word means a place of amusement, wherein there shall be a theater, some wax figures, a giant and dwarf or two, a jumble of pictures, and a few live snakes." But that combination suited the public just fine, and fairs were already bringing the museum's main drawing cards to millions of people in the American heartland.

A midget named Charles Sherwood was a headliner when P. T. Barnum exhibited him—as "General Tom Thumb"—at the New York State Fair at Saratoga Springs in the fall of 1847. Not bad for a nine-year-old from Bridgeport, Connecticut (where Barnum later served as mayor). At 31 inches tall and 70 pounds, Sherwood was not particularly small for a midget, but he loomed large in the world of entertainment. Historians of popular culture

agree that he was a bona fide celebrity, one of the best-known men of his era. He grew wealthy, and by the end of his career, 20 million people had viewed him. Such was his renown that when he married a dwarf, Lavinia Warren, in 1863, President Abraham Lincoln received the couple at the White House.

Even though a midget could shake hands with the president, carnival freak shows were anathema to ministers, matrons, community leaders, and other self-appointed watchdogs who fretted about the morals of local citizens and the respectability of their community. Nothing testifies to the popularity of snake boys and bearded ladies—not to mention cooch dancers, gamblers, and bootleggers—as eloquently as the persistent efforts, spanning decades, to get rid of them.

Freak shows proved both durable and creative. When the rise of vaudeville drew patrons from museums, the human oddities joined circus sideshows, becoming an integral part of them during their golden age from 1870 to 1920. When the Barnum & Bailey Circus toured England in 1898, it brought a troupe of 30 freaks, including the Moss-Haired Girl, the Double-Bodied Wonder, the Armless Girl, and the India Rubber Man. When films, amusement parks, and radio took audiences away from circuses in the 1920s, freaks signed on with traveling carnivals.

Managers of fairs earnestly tried to clean up their acts, but their efforts often proved futile. Carnival operators paid lip service to morality and honesty, but disreputable shows materialized anyway. Planning the 1870 Indiana State Fair, superintendent John Sullivan banned an impressive list of sideshows, including fat women, "white Negroes," and snake handlers. "They bring in their trail the worst classes of thieves and scoundrels of low and high degree," Sullivan asserted. "Besides, no good emanates from their exhibitions." Strong words, yet sideshows were back on the Indiana fairgrounds a year later. In 1872 the Indiana fair board again banned them; again it must have been fruitless, because five years later, fair annals reveal new efforts to get rid of a fat woman, a five-legged calf and a snake handler with a boa constrictor. In 1909 fair planners demanded the prohibition of "monstrosities," as they would regularly during the ensuing decades, all the way until 1951, when the Cetlin and Wilson Carnival's midway at the Indiana State Fair featured—you guessed it—a freak show.

Fair managers in other states were in a similar quandary. Freak shows were admittedly seamy, even repulsive, but they were also lucrative (sideshow operators paid $150 apiece for spots on the midway at fairs in the 1870s). Banished outside a fair's tall, wooden fence, they still made plenty of money, except the fair didn't get its share. Furthermore, plenty of people genuinely enjoyed the freak shows and saw nothing wrong with them. As the secretary of a Pennsylvania county agricultural association once noted, the group's bylaws prohibited sideshows (along with gambling, horse racing, and games of chance), but the pressure for what he called "a little nonsense now and then" was almost irresistible.

Efforts to oust freaks from the midway probably added to their bizarre allure. Supply increased to meet demand. Such was Gen. Tom Thumb's renown that numerous imitators arrived on the scene, including midgets who predictably called themselves Colonel Small, Commodore Nutt, and Commodore Foote. Troupes of midgets appeared in reviews, where they danced, sang, tumbled, and told jokes. The genre reached its zenith at the 1934 Chicago World's Fair, where a veteran sideshow operator and barker named Nate Eagle put together an elaborate midget city inhabited by 187 of the little people. Eagle had honed his carnie talents during the 1920s with the James E. Strates Shows, the World of Mirth, and the Royal American Shows, companies that provided carnival midways for many state fairs. In Chicago, Eagle outdid himself. Fair visitors could eat in a midget café and get haircuts in a midget barbershop. Motorists could buy gasoline in a tiny filling station; vendors sold miniature newspapers for a nickel. The attraction was one of the biggest moneymakers of the fair.

Freak shows were so numerous and well-established that a formal pay scale developed, tied to specific deformities, glandular conditions, and diseases. In 1935 average salaries ranged from $25 to $125 per week; this pat scale offers an unusual insight into the peculiar tastes of freak-show fans. At the low end was the human skeleton (sometimes known as the "cigarette fiend"). Fat men earned $30 a week; fat women, such as Ruth Pontico, billed as the "world's fattest dancer" at fairs in the 1940s, earned up to $50. Pontico's promotional material pegged her at weights ranging from 700 to 800 pounds, mentioned her 37-inch arms, and sometimes called her "Baby Ruth, the fattest woman in the world."

Perhaps fat women were more versatile or creative than fat men: some combined their bulk with tattoos, doubling their midway allure. Carrie Akers of Virginia was a 300-pound dwarf, just 35 inches tall. Curiously, the banners advertising fat ladies often contained elements of eroticism, showing them lifting their skirts or wearing flimsy, revealing dresses.

Extreme hairiness was another desirable oddity. Bearded ladies commanded up to $75 a week. They shared the appeal of another of Barnum's famous freaks: Theodore Peteroff, famous as Jo-Jo the Dog-Faced Boy.

Also known as "the Human Skye Terrier," he had long, soft hair on his cheeks, face, and forehead.

Giants, earning $80 a week, were often touted as having been born in exotic places or as members of unusual ethnic groups. The Indiana State Fair of 1853 featured the Kickapoo Giantess (supposedly a member of a North American Indian tribe that lived in the territory from Illinois to Wisconsin). Dozens of "Peruvian" giants appeared at various fairs and carnivals, although, as a contemporary writer observed, they were more likely from Lima, Ohio, or Lima, Illinois, than Lima, Peru.

The highest-paid freak of the 1935 season was a baby with four legs, who earned $125 a week for a 30-week tour. For some reason, vestigial limbs were a must-see for the myriad aficionados of freaks. At the 1950 Michigan State Fair, a girl with four legs was nothing less than a "top midway attraction," according to news accounts. The young, studious-looking black woman was a sophomore at a Georgia college who worked carnivals in the summer. Her two extra "legs" were attached to her hips. Author Walter Graham may have had her partly in mind when he wrote, in his 1953 book *Monster Midway*, "The best draw is a girl who had three legs or arms or a woman with parts of another body sprouting from her waist."

All of these human oddities drew paychecks, although one carnie figured out how to employ some freaks for free. In the 1950s, sideshow operator Louis "Duke" Jeanette offered an attraction called "Mystery of Birth—World's Strangest Babies": a collection of more than two dozen deformed embryos and fetuses, including one that had two

The flimsy outfit on "Dolly Dimple" in these banners adds an unexpected erotic element that was typical in fat-lady posters. These banners were photographed at a festival in Plant City, Florida, in 1939. Marion Post Wolcott/Library of Congress, LC-USF-33-30477-M4

"The best draw is a girl who had three legs or arms or a woman with parts of another body sprouting from her waist."
—WALTER GRAHAM, FROM HIS 1953 BOOK *MONSTER MIDWAY*.

**This fat lady added a twist to her corpulent charms, according to a poster that appeared at the 1941 Vermont State Fair.** Jack Delano/Library of Congress, LC-USF35-44

faces, one with four arms, another with four legs, and one that looked like a gorilla. Jeanette dodged questions about the exact sources of his exhibits, but he revealed that he'd paid doctors as much as $1,000 for some of them.

At the Gratz Fair in Pennsylvania in 1958, patrons could see the Pickled Punks, described in a contemporary article as "two questionable sets of Siamese twins preserved in formaldehyde." They shared the bill with a hermaphrodite named Carmelita and Devil, the Two-Nosed Dog.

This observation that a freak was "questionable" underlines the fact that some freaks weren't genuine. Showmen weren't above improving on nature if they had to. Artful presentation, the linguistic skill of the barker, and canny publicity were often enough to generate a cascade of dimes at the ticket booth, even for attractions that now seem palpably phony. In the 1840s, the best-known early museum (Peale's in Baltimore) exhibited Barnum's legendary "Fejee mermaid," the upper torso of a monkey stitched to the body and tail of a large fish. Sixty years later, "pickled mermaids" were still drawing curious, gullible crowds.

Hermaphrodites like Carmelita, mentioned above, were other popular but highly suspect attractions, billed as "half-man, half-woman," elaborately costumed and made up to look the part. On stage, they were often presented so that one profile was a bearded, muscular male, and the other a female with a prominent breast. However, doctors unanimously deny such a possibility. Although there have been rare cases of people who have both ovaries and testicles, this biological oddity isn't otherwise reflected in their appearance.

One of the earliest giantesses touring fairs, billed as "Madame Gomez, the tallest woman in the world," was just six feet tall. She wore high heels and a billowy dress; during her show, the pitchman summoned the tallest man from the audience to come up and walk under her outstretched arm. As the volunteer climbed to the stage, Madame Gomez slowly stepped back, as if to make room, up onto a concealed shelf that added 6 inches to her height. Her dress hid the maneuver. Male giants were often not much more than 6 feet tall, either, but they favored huge boots containing 6-inch lifts and 2-foot-tall hats.

Faced with eager, unsophisticated audiences, carnies found that their audacity and cleverness rarely went unrewarded. A tongue-in-cheek article in *American Mercury* magazine once praised sideshow operators for their ingenuity in the "unearthing of bogus phenomena." The author traced the first American sideshow to southern Ohio, where it had "as its nickel-luring attraction what was said to be the only Negro albino in captivity, the said Negro albino being actually nothing more peculiar than a small colored boy in a blond wig." (These bizarre attractions were sometimes billed as the Man From Mars or the Man From the Moon).

Mademoiselle Fanny, a fat girl, weighed a mere 210 pounds but strapped metal bars beneath her tent-like robe when she climbed on a scale on stage to document her corpulence.

A filthy, gibbering "wild man" called Zup, billed as the Missing Link, was actually a high-school graduate who made extra money writing for a well-known entertainment tabloid. Many of the early wild men were supposedly from Borneo, an island in the Malay Archipelago that sounded authentically distant and primitive, like Timbuktu. After the Spanish-American War in 1898, they quickly began hailing from the Philippines, as sideshow owners capitalized on the public's interest in our new colonial possession. They were usually exhibited in a cage gnawing on large bones. Eyeing one such specimen, a customer once noticed an eagle tattooed on the wild man's arm, which spoiled the primitive effect. Another member of the audience observed that the wild man had been a barber before he became a Filipino.

Wild men, billed as Congo the Gorilla Man or Bosco, were a common attraction, invariably phony. One show exhibited a so-called wild man, allegedly trapped in the jungles of South America, hidden in a canvas pen; the barker punctuated his talk by jabbing a metal trident into the enclosure, while explaining that the government was about to transport the creature to Washington for experiments. But, as Arthur Ruhl wrote in *Collier's*, it was actually "a boy, inexpressibly bored, with a long-haired wig, and face and arms carelessly daubed with burnt cork."

Nate Eagle foisted numerous bogus attractions on the unsuspecting public during his long career. His exploits might have gone unrecorded were it not for two long interviews by Robert L. Taylor in the *New Yorker* in 1952. Taylor described Eagle as "a carnival talker of almost unparalleled genius, a man of such deep, legitimate guile and persuasion that, over the past 43 years, with acts too varied and spurious to list fully, he has probably hoodwinked at least half the nation."

Eagle recounted how he had once spieled for a two-headed baby. He installed a pair of loudspeakers, apparently wired to microphones inside the tent, and over which the crowd heard two distinctly different cries. The two-headed baby, Eagle announced during his brilliant monologue, was "the most amazing and provocative phenomenon ever offered by this or any other amusement center in the world." After paying their dimes, however, visitors discovered that the baby was made of rubber. When they complained, Eagle acted shocked and amazed. "Why, I thought you understood that it was an authentic rubber baby," he

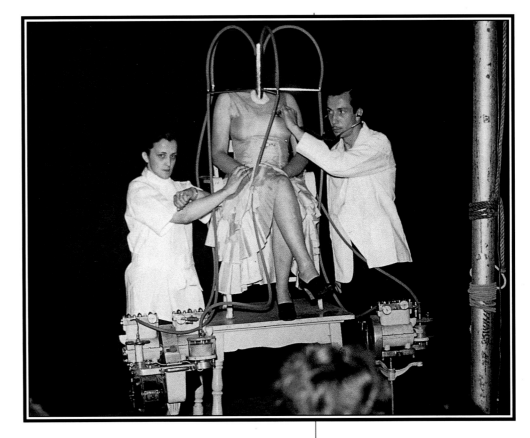

told them. "There isn't any such thing as a live two-headed baby; grown-up people ought to know that."

The rubes were usually too embarrassed to get angry, or else they were laughing at having been bilked by a master. Fred Beckman, who ran a carnival in St. Louis, once told Eagle, "You have all the ingredients necessary to rise in your profession—a deceptively honest face, a genius for legitimate fraud, no conscience, a golden tongue, and a feeling that a quarter in somebody else's pocket is a personal rebuke."

An element of fraud seemed par for the course in freak shows. Ted Evans, well-known as the English Giant, was quite tall (probably close to 7 feet), but advertisements claimed that he was 9 feet 6 inches tall. When freaks were authentic (if perhaps exaggerated), showmen had to try to convince a skeptical public that the attractions were both real and animate; thus, the word "alive" became an important part of a sideshow banner.

For most freaks, unfortunately, their afflictions required no exaggeration beyond an imaginative name. In the 1950s, an Alligator Boy was a star of Claude Bentley's Freak Circus, which traveled with the James E. Strates Shows. His name was William Parnell, born in 1925 in Kenly, North Carolina. Parnell suffered from an

**Although not part of a freak show per se, the famous "headless lady" (here presented by the Rubin and Cherry midway company at the 1940 Iowa State Fair) was a classic of its type. The torso was usually attended by a "doctor" and a "nurse," and apparently animated by whatever noisy, complicated, salvaged machinery the sideshow company could scrape together. The performers often acted as if only their personal attendance kept the headless body alive.**
Iowa State Fair–Des Moines

**An alligator boy was among the human odd-ities at the 1941 Vermont State Fair. The ride in the foreground was a version of the popular Loop-O-Plane.** Jack Delano/Library of Congress, LC-USF-35-51

> "A carnival talker of almost unparalleled genius, a man of such deep, legitimate guile and persuasion that, over the past 43 years, with acts too varied and spurious to list fully, he has probably hoodwinked at least half the nation."
>
> —WRITER ROBERT L. TAYLOR DESCRIBING NATE EAGLE, *NEW YORKER*, 1952.

**Curious crowds could meet the mother of these genetic rarities at the 1941 Vermont State Fair in Rutland. Note that the barker is dressed as a "nurse" to add a nebulous medical aura to a sideshow that depended for its impact on the scandalous fact that Mrs. Armstrong had obviously had sex almost simultaneously with a white man and a black man. The large word "alive" repeated at right was, according to sideshow sign painters, the most important word in their arsenal.** Library of Congress, LC-USF-33-21133-M1

obscure skin disease that left him covered with greenish-white patches, a condition that most people agreed looked distinctly reptilian. He was so repellent that the local school refused to admit him; as a result, he ran away and joined a carnival at age nine. "I don't mind when they look at me; that's what I get paid for," he told a magazine writer in 1952. "But then they ask me, is it a fake? Really, I wish it was a fake."

Whether they were real or fake, alive or embalmed, freaks gradually disappeared from state fair midways during the 1950s, victims of changing times and public attitudes. World War II posed logistical problems, according to Fred Smythe, who managed prewar sideshows. Smythe employed hundreds of freaks during his career, making him an excellent commentator on the demise of the genre. And he looked the part. In a 1942 article in the *New Yorker*, writer Mark Murphy described Smythe as a "chunky fellow with a square, authoritative face," and wearing a black-and-white pencil-striped suit, a green hat with the brim turned down in front, sporting a diamond ring on his right pinky and chewing a fat cigar. Smythe observed that World War II had been bad for business, because so many midgets came from Austria and Germany. Many tattooed people and giants were European, as well.

Smythe was excited about his postwar prospects, especially a giant that he had his eyes on, allegedly 8 feet 4 inches tall. Smythe's giant, unfortunately, had gotten stuck in the Finnish Army, and Smythe was worried that he would be such a large target that the enemy would find it easy to shoot him. But Smythe fully expected the giant to pull down $300 a week, and another $100 selling photos, after the war.

But larger problems loomed on the horizon, less transitory than world war. "This country isn't producing freaks so much anymore," Smythe told Murphy. "These sanitary codes and health laws have a lot to do with it. Improve the public health and they beget fewer monsters. You get sanitary codes, and you don't get many three-legged and two-bodied people."

Smythe had run afoul of modern medicine at least once, when he had employed a midget named Col. Tiny. A severe illness put the Colonel in a hospital, where doctors began treating him for a pituitary gland problem. After treatment, Smythe complained, Col. Tiny started to grow. "He don't grow big enough to be a man, but he grows big enough to where he isn't a very good midget," Smythe said, shaking his head. "You would figure a doctor, a fellow with a college education, would have more sense."

Anyway, Smythe admitted, the public was losing its taste for freaks who were too weird and disgusting. Crowds had become uncomfortable gaping at people with serious deformities or birth defects, such as Selo the Seal-Boy, who had no arms, just "flippers." Some conditions were painful, which made them considerably less entertaining for audiences with a shred of sensitivity. Smythe once employed a thin man from Maspeth, New York, who was 6 feet tall and weighed 65 pounds. "Thin men, good ones, who are just a framework of bones with skin stretched over them, usually have a hard time walking," Smythe pointed out. "Can't go upstairs." Sometimes their thinness stemmed from an advanced case of tuberculosis.

Doctors dispelled part of the mystique that surrounded freaks by providing down-to-earth diagnoses. The Blue Man had overdosed on silver nitrate, once an ingredient in medicine for stomach ulcers. The Ugliest Woman in the World suffered from acromegaly, which grossly enlarges the jaw, nose, lips, and tongue. The Boy with the Cigar-Shaped Head was microcephalic. Such people deserved medical care and therapy, not gaping rubes and public displays of revulsion. And fair managers had, as a group, renewed their dedication to providing wholesome, family entertainment.

Among the veteran carnies, though, old attitudes died hard, as evidenced by an article in *Time* magazine on Sept. 29, 1958. Helen Alter, whose husband ran the Gratz Fair in Pennsylvania, complained: "You can't get good freaks anymore. Seems like they're all dying off." Her husband, Lew, agreed: " 'They take 'em and put 'em in an institution now,' he moaned. 'They don't want 'em exposed. Now I ain't going to mention any names, but I know an insane asylum where there's three good pinheads right now. But you can't get them out.' "

Such comments raised the question of who should have been in the asylum. Whether freaks were happier in an institution or on the road earning money was rapidly

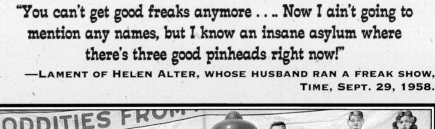

"You can't get good freaks anymore . . . . Now I ain't going to mention any names, but I know an insane asylum where there's three good pinheads right now!"
—LAMENT OF HELEN ALTER, WHOSE HUSBAND RAN A FREAK SHOW, TIME, SEPT. 29, 1958.

By 1968, when this photo was taken at the Oklahoma State Fair, freak shows were on their way out. This one tries hard, though, with a full assortment of sword swallowers, a rubber man, a pinhead midget, and what seems to be a frog boy. State Fair of Oklahoma

becoming moot, in any case. The public was becoming better educated and more enlightened. The days when a midway could bill a black midget as a "Tree-Climbing Pygmy" or advertise a wild-man act as "Ubangi Savages" were ending.

By modern standards, a few of the old freaks now seem tame. Consider the 14-year-old tattooed lady from the 1940 edition of the Buckeye State Shows. Her smattering of tattoos included a picture of Christ wearing the crown of thorns on her right thigh. Back then, that was enough to earn her a spot on the midway. Today, you can see athletes with more body art at college basketball games on television. Body piercing, too, has become mainstream.

Nowadays the genre, once a mainstay of midways across the country, has just about vanished, the result of changing attitudes and tastes. The World's Smallest Woman still makes the rounds of state fairs, but it is doubtful whether she or anyone in her audiences has ever heard of Gen. Tom Thumb, who was received by European royalty and once dined with Honest Abe himself. She is a fitting, faint echo of the weird, hilarious, disturbing saga of freak shows at the fair.

# CHAPTER TEN

# Holding On to History

"New" or "improved" described many exhibits—both animal and mechanical—at the first fairs. It wasn't long before "old" and "classic" applied to another sort of display. The initial focus on invention was soon counterbalanced by a concern with capturing the rapidly vanishing past. Fairs, which began as a cram course in the modern, soon added a variety of history lessons to their curricula.

As early as 1878, the Indiana State Fair was already hosting a special event for old-timers from the state's early days, "when pluck and undaunted courage were the crowning virtues," in the words of a contemporary writer. Pioneers who were more than 70 years old and had lived in the state for 40 years could attend for free; 700 took advantage of the offer. A few could no doubt recall Gen. William Henry Harrison's victory over Tecumseh at the Battle of Tippecanoe in 1811, which opened the territory for lasting settlement.

At the 1904 Iowa fair, fairgoers strolled past transportation history in the form of oxcarts, a prairie schooner, Conestoga wagons, and a stage-coach. Accounts of the fair noted that older men in the crowd remembered seeing these vehicles during the early years of statehood. Also on exhibit was an early model of McCormick's reaper, a design that required one man to walk along behind it, raking. Later designs had a place for a man to ride as he raked. Displays of spinning wheels, flintlock muskets, flax hackles, and hand-powered corn grinders elicited comments such as, "Why, we've got one like that at home" and "I can remember that!" from the crowd.

"To many, it seemed odd that the old, familiar objects in their own home should now be classed as an important part of the picture of the history of Iowa."
—VISITOR TO HISTORICAL DISPLAYS AT IOWA'S "DIAMOND JUBILEE FAIR," 1904.

A memorable part of the historical displays was what one historian called the "real pioneers of Iowa": the original plants of the prairie. There was "slough grass that pioneers used to turn rain from their roofs, tall bluestem or 'turkey toe,' switch grass, that fed oxen and horses in the early winters. Here were straight-stalked, bushy-leaved, prairie clover and the purple-blossomed plant that went by the same name. Here was the ox-eyed daisy, goldenrod, black-eyed Susan, wild sunflower; here was blue vervain, the vetch-like partridge pea, the familiar ironweed, and tickle grass."

The Iowa State Fair found a unique way to explore the state's agricultural history by displaying crops that were once common but had become mostly abandoned. Gazing at the colorful leaves and showy flower heads of amaranth, older residents got a chance to see a crop they remembered from their youth, while youngsters got to learn about a plant they may have never heard of. Other crops on display included buckwheat, oil rapeseed (grown as a forage for cattle), flax, safflower, lupine, and foxtail millet.

A section of the Tunbridge World's Fair in Vermont was called Antique Hill. It featured a collection of old household furnishings, kitchen implements, and workshop tools. A local resident, Ed Flint, started it in

Fairs carefully preserved, dramatized, and explained local history with a colorful variety of exhibits. This sod house, built by prairie-dwellers who lacked wood, drew curious visitors to the Iowa State Fair in August 1968. Scarce lumber was used for rafters, window frames, and doors. Iowa State Fair, Des Moines

COLISEUM BUILDING, EASTERN STATES EXPOSITION, SPRINGFIELD, MASS.

The caption for this postcard mentions that the Eastern States Exposition covered a tract of 172 acres, the largest fairground in the East, and that 250,000 people attended each year. The fair had accommodations for 1,200 cattle, 600 horses, 1,000 sheep and swine, and more than 100,000 square feet of general exhibition space under roof. Eastern States Exposition

the 1920s when he recognized how quickly technology was making obsolete the familiar things of the recent past. He began collecting the sperm oil lamps and lard squeezers that were being discarded, seeing in these simple domestic items a way to make young people and newcomers appreciate the difficulties and devices of earlier generations. Hard-working housewives had no particular fondness for the wooden washboard and the hand-cranked wringer, cheerfully pitching these things onto the scrap heap when electricity had been enlisted into the incessant war against dirty laundry. But wasn't it interesting, 30 years later, to view those very things, to explain to a grandchild how they worked (or, more likely, how you worked), and to explore the shortcomings of the good old days? As Ed Flint foresaw, the laborious, inefficient devices that new inventions aimed to get rid of gradually turned into popular displays that evoked curiosity and nostalgia.

Such is the age of some of the oldest permanent fairgrounds (Minnesota, 1885; New York, 1890; Indiana, 1892) that buildings originally erected as the latest in magnificent architecture (aimed at impressing visitors and glorifying the host state) gradually acquired historical status. The Exposition Building at the Illinois State Fair was built in 1894. The Ohio fairground, which dates from 1883, still has structures built in 1888: the North Commercial Building, the Antique and Collectibles Pavilion, and the Rabbit and Poultry Building. Other old structures, such as the Agriculture Building (built in 1904) and the Sheep Barn (1917) are what a contemporary description termed "priceless examples of classic, exposition-style architecture." The fair preserved a barn that had stood on the land that became the fairground in 1886. Restored in the early 1970s, it once housed antique farm equipment displays.

Pioneer Hall at the Iowa fairground (which is a year newer than Ohio's) was built in 1886, and originally housed poultry. Its ceiling is an intricate trestlework of dark wooden beams. Curved windows high on its old brick walls allow sunlight to flood the exhibitions below. The Livestock Pavilion at the Iowa fairground was patterned after one in Scotland. That fair possesses a 1915 Sheep Barn decorated with 34 *bas-relief* busts of rams' heads, on a blue tile background with

"Why, we've got one like that at home!" ... "I can remember that!"
—EXCLAMATIONS FROM THE CROWD AT IOWA'S "DIAMOND JUBILEE FAIR," 1904.

Farmers examine old plows and farm implements at the Tunbridge World's Fair in Vermont, September 1941. In a few generations, plows went from the stars of the show to historical curiosities. Jack Delano/Library of Congress, LC-USF-45767-D

Exposition Building,
Iowa State Fair Grounds, Des Moines, Iowa.

**The fine old Exposition Building, built in 1885 at the Iowa fairground, was torn down in 1950 because it had become a fire hazard. A contemporary newspaper article described the building as "fancywork and romance headquarters" of the fair.** Iowa State Fair—Des Moines

**The Ohio Centennial Exposition in 1888 celebrated the 100th year (1788–1888) of the state's first permanent settlement, which resulted from the Northwest Ordinance of 1787. The 46-day event took the place of the fair that year, although it included all of the usual events and attractions.** Ohio Expositions Commission and C. LaVon Shook

green leaves beneath. Large triptychs of scenes of sheep in pasture flank the entrance. Flowered tiles line the sides of the entrance; the building's name appears on an arch overhead, carved in formal, bank-style letters.

Moving west, the age of what constitutes "historical" changes a bit. The Arizona State Fair has at least one building that was erected for the 1905 fair, the Floriculture Building (originally the Mining Building). In all, the fair still makes use of four buildings that pre-date Arizona's statehood.

Some fairs acquired significant buildings from other locations. After the World's Columbian Exhibition of 1893 in Chicago, a domed building from the grounds was disassembled and erected at the Illinois state fairground in 1895. Valued at $200,000, it was heralded as the "second largest unsupported dome in the world." It served as the fair's horticultural center until in burned down in August 1917, just before the fair opened. The California State Fair's Hall of Flowers is a modernistic building that originally came from the 1939–1940 San Francisco's World's Fair.

Members of 4-H clubs show cattle at the South Dakota State Fair's 4-H Beef Barn, which was built in 1913. Fans who fill the grandstand for races and rodeos find themselves sitting in a structure that dates from 1918.

Some old buildings have found new incarnations. The Illinois fair's Poultry Building, which was built in

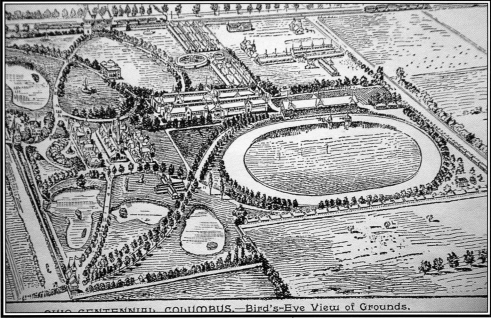

OHIO CENTENNIAL COLUMBUS.—Bird's-Eye View of Grounds.

1896 and once held 2,000 coops of prize fowl, now houses tools and supplies used in maintaining the fairground. Minnesota's 1907 Dairy Building contains an arts center, but Ye Olde Mill, the fair's oldest ride, retains the same gentle appeal that it possessed in 1913, when couples first sluiced along its dark waterway.

This time-ravaged poster shows the layout of the fifth Ohio State Fair, held in 1854 in Newark. Fair dates were changed that year because of an outbreak of Asian cholera. Ohio Expositions Commission and C. LaVon Shook

This information booth at the Ohio fairground is one of the fair's two oldest buildings. It was erected in 1888 as a food stand for the state's centennial celebration. Ohio Expositions Commission and C. LaVon Shook

Many fairs have created special exhibits aimed at preserving and explaining regional history. On the grounds of the Eastern States Exposition in Massachusetts is Storrowton Village Museum, which re-creates New England life during the 1800s. The site was the brainstorm of Helen Osborne Storrow, wife of a Boston millionaire and banker. She became the first woman to serve on the Exposition's Board of Trustees, and was a pioneer in historic preservation. Mrs. Storrow began the village by having an old farmhouse moved to the fairground in 1927. There eventually followed a steepled meetinghouse from 1834 (originally in Salisbury, New Hampshire, and now a popular site for weddings), a restaurant spliced together from an 18th-century tavern and a 19th-century Baptist meeting house, an 1810 schoolhouse, a lawyer's office, and a blacksmith shop. The village is open year-round for tours and activities, including day camps during the summer.

In 1956 the Utah State Fair transported a Mormon village exhibit to the fair to help celebrate the fair's

"You ought to be down here and see all the horse and cattle," tourist Willie Seltenreich wrote on this postcard in 1915. "They sure are great."

The Ohio fairground, circa 1909. The grand structure at left was built around 1888 as a women's building. It was replaced in 1909 by a new women's building, since renamed the **Cox Fine Arts Center.** Ohio Expositions Commission and C. LaVon Shook

Bird's Eye View Iowa State Fair Grounds, Agricultural Bldg. in fore ground, Des Moines, Iowa.

State Fair Grounds. Columbus, Ohio.

**The Poultry-Rabbit Building at the Ohio State Fair.** Ohio State Fair

centennial. In 1959 the Oregon State Fair created what it called the Centennial Farmstead, a model farm of the 1850s, with a two-room cabin containing antique furniture, an implement shed, and a well, surrounded by a rail fence. As a way of personalizing history that year, the fair sponsored a contest for what it called the "oldest centennial article"; the winner submitted a calico dress that had been worn by her great-grandmother in the 1820s. Other fairs devised similar categories; the Indiana State Fair in 1950 held a contest for the best collection of Indian relics, Civil War bedspreads, and shawls.

The Utah State Fair's Mountain Man Village and the Wyoming State Fair's Pioneer Memorial Museum are similar efforts at keeping history fresh. In 1934 the Indiana fair built a model of a modern school and, for comparison purposes, a representation of a school from a century earlier, a one-room, log schoolhouse circa 1834. Fairgoers watched a costumed schoolmaster and students simulate antique lessons. At its Heritage Circle, the North Carolina State Fair also displays an 18th-century schoolhouse.

Although the exterior of Hook's Historic Drug Store at the Indiana State Fair is less than 40 years old, it houses an authentic replica of a late–nineteenth century Indiana drugstore, full of curiosities from the heyday of patent medicine. Hook's features an 1875 soda fountain that still works (the ornate glass "fountain" that lent the device its name has been removed, unfortunately). Ornate, wooden wall fixtures and counters

**One of the most distinctive buildings at the old California State Fairground was the Agriculture Pavilion, built in 1918.** California State Fair

line the store; they were built in 1852 for a druggist in Cambridge City, Indiana, and are rich with carvings, curves, and elaborate moldings.

Many of the pharmacy and drugstore antiques in Hook's were collected by the family of E. H. Bindley, a wholesale druggist in Terre Haute, starting in 1865. Ten-foot-tall, glass-fronted cabinets and crowded shelves contain quart jars of ink from the pre-ballpoint-pen days, hand rollers for "pill dough," vending machines for penny stamps, bars of carbolic soap, straight razors, Canada Snake-Root, and a medicine called Sa-Tan-Ic Laxative (the label shows a devil).

At the Indiana Fair's Pioneer Village, visitors watch women making quilts and lace, candle makers working with golden beeswax, and a carver making solid wooden bowls. The Village building includes a room that re-creates the Summer Kitchen, "A light and airy place for cooking, canning and ironing," according to a sign. "It was about 80 degrees out here, if the wind was blowing."

Already deeply involved in historical reenactments, the Indiana fair is building a 23-acre addition to its fairground that will house a museum called the Center for Agricultural Science and Heritage in a 1934 barn. Barn connoisseurs may want to visit just to see the barn itself; it's a beautiful structure built by a wealthy Indiana farmer who didn't have to cut any corners during construction.

During fair week, one end of the Indiana fairground percolates with colorful and sometimes noisy displays. A field of antique tractors includes a 1913 Avery that still runs; it is one of only three or four in the United States. Nearby are Olivers and red Farm-Alls, reddish-orange Allis-Chalmers, and red-and-gray Fords.

Hard-working housewives had no particular fondness for the wooden washboard and the hand-cranked wringer. . . . But wasn't it interesting, 30 years later, to view those very things, to explain to a grandchild how they worked, and to explore the shortcomings of the good old days?

Perhaps no single word, barring perhaps "Alive!" or "Free!" excited so many fairgoers as the word "modern." The hutch at left is, of course, now a staple of antique stores. An ad for a local plumber peeks from under the sink. This exhibit was at the Georgia State Exposition in Macon, Georgia, in 1928. Georgia Department of Archives and History

Wayne Dillman, a retired teacher and farmer, does the honors at a demonstration of the history of threshing at the 1998 Indiana State Fair. Volunteers start by showing how to use a flail, then work their way through generations of technology.

Before powerful, mobile gasoline tractors took over, some farmers used steam engines like this 1924 Case to run large, complex implements. This engine drives a 1900 Red River threshing machine at the 1998 Indiana State Fair.

Some tractors are battered and rusty; others have been restored to showroom condition. Tractor lovers will enjoy the 1921 Rumely Oil Pull, with its steel wheels and an engine that runs on kerosene.

Burning coal and belching steam is a half-size Gar-Scott steam engine, an exact replica of a 1915 original. Nearby is a 1924 Case steam engine (one of the last ones built) that volunteers use to run a huge, belt-driven, 1900 Red River threshing machine during an afternoon program that reenacts the history of harvesting grain. One volunteer, clad in blue overalls, demonstrates how to use a flail; another operates a hand-cranked machine that separates wheat from chaff. A later stage in harvesting involves a 1929 Allis-Chalmers gasoline tractor, which has taken over the running of the belt to the thresher.

The Iowa fairground is also studded with historical buildings and displays, including an old "basement barn" of the kind originally built into hillsides. With stone foundations, these barns were cooler in summer and warmer in winter. Chatting with a visitor, I found that he had recently lost a century-old basement barn on his farm, toppled by a violent storm.

A popular part of the historical reenactments at the Indiana State Fair is a demonstration of one of the earliest forms of farmyard power, the ox team.

The Minnesota State Fair possesses one of the most thematically appropriate museum buildings in America: a refurbished carnival car donated by Royal American Shows, which supplied the fair's carnival and midway for 60 years. The car, and several other buildings, are packed with artifacts and memorabilia. Minnesota State Fair

The Iowa fair even has a museum dedicated to its own impressive history. On display are an old ticket booth and turnstile, a wooden bench from the Women's Building, and a seat from the old grandstand. Elsewhere is a bell from one of the locomotives wrecked during a spectacular thrill show in 1896. You can prop your foot on the performing stand used by the elephant named "Mine," purchased in the 1920s when 15,000 Iowa boys and girls contributed pennies, nickels, and dimes to a public campaign that raised $3,600. She was christened on the opening day of the fair in 1927. Fair press releases carefully reported on her progress, noting that she weighed 1,160 pounds in 1929, and was up to 3,500 pounds when she embarked on a tour of the state in 1934. Using her stand—a 30-inch-square steel frame topped by a 2-inch wooden slab—"Mine" did tricks for school children during her annual birthday party at the fair.

The Museum of State Fair History at the Minnesota State Fair is built around brightly painted and fully restored carnival train cars donated by Royal American Shows, which supplied the fair's carnival and midway from 1933 until 1994. The cluster of memorabilia contains the old North St. Paul train depot and switch tower, which were moved to the fairground in 1976. Speedy's Garage, also called "The Car Crash Museum," contains

The interior of the Minnesota State Fair's carnival train car at the fair's museum. Thanks to foresight and dedicated volunteers, the Minnesota fair has managed to preserve an extraordinary amount of its own colorful history. Minnesota State Fair

The Minnesota State Fair's museum includes buildings from the fair's old automotive garage and train station. Minnesota State Fair

INDIAN HEAD FROM "OLD" WOMEN'S BUILDING

Some old fairground buildings, needless to say, have succumbed to time and the wrecking ball during the years. This bust decorated the old Women's Building at the Minnesota State Fair, and now graces the fair's museum. Minnesota State Fair

TICKET DISPENSER

OLD TIME TICKET BOX

Minnesota STATE FAIR

TICKET TAKER'S BOX and APRON

Only the ticket booth stood between fairgoers and their day packed with fun. This may have been the one place that every fairgoer visited. Minnesota State Fair

a pair of old race cars, and was modeled after turn-of-the-century facilities used by the pioneer automobile racers on the fairground track. There's a room devoted to grandstand entertainment through the years, containing artifacts, posters, and sideshow props; a railroad baggage car devoted to ice shows; and a caboose. The blacksmith shop, built in 1937, was used during the last decade of horse racing at the fair; some of its wood came from the old swine and horse barns of the late 1800s.

Gale Frost, the amiable curator of the complex, started at the fair in 1921 when he was eight years old, working as a lemonade mixer in his father's refreshment stand. His father went on to become a member of the State Fair's Hall of Fame, an honor that seems guaranteed for Gale, as well.

Everything at fairs seems to eventually come full circle. At the first Minnesota fair, in 1860, one of the most popular contests involved fire companies. The winning crew threw a stream of water 200 feet. For many spectators, it was the first time they had seen a fire engine at work. Nearly a century later, the 1953 Eastern States Exposition held an old-fashioned "firemen's muster," featuring century-old, manually operated pumps. Once again, it was probably the first time many in the audience had seen such devices.

Trunks full of memories from a cavalcade of performers who have taken their final curtain calls are exhibited at the Minnesota State Fair museum. Minnesota State Fair

# CHAPTER ELEVEN

# Something for Everyone

Before the Civil War, agricultural fairs aimed at audiences of male farmers; traveling was hard and costly, two good reasons not to bring along the whole family. Wives and children weren't all that fascinated by new plow designs and theories about manure, anyway. Nevertheless, some of the first organizers of fairs felt that the events should involve the whole family.

Massachusetts agrarian and businessman Elkanah Watson, often described as "the father of the American fair" (see chapter 2), believed that men and women alike could benefit from fairs, which he saw as educational opportunities. He determined that domestic work and fine arts and crafts should be recognized, yet he had trouble convincing women to attend. They weren't used to taking part in organized activities in public places, where the definition of "ladylike" was extraordinarily strict. To dissolve this resistance, Watson organized genteel "pastoral balls" in the evenings during the fair. He provided a nonthreatening milieu by holding award ceremonies in a town's largest church. To show that the events were respectable, he asked his wife to present the ribbons won by women in the domestic categories of the competition.

Because fair organizers always wanted to boost attendance, Watson's line of reasoning was logical. In the 1850s and 1860s, many state fairs admitted "members" on the first two days, charging them a dollar apiece, then dropping the price and offering "family tickets." A special "children's day" became a standard feature, offering reduced fees for kids, and sometimes letting them in for free.

> "To meet friends, to eat taffy, to see the automobile races, to hear speeches, to watch plays, to ride roller-coasters and to have general non-professional fun."
> —REASONS TO ATTEND THE IOWA STATE FAIR, TIME, 1935.

Following Watson's lead, fairs offered awards in a wide variety of demonstrations, displays, and contests that had little to do with agriculture. The 1850 Ohio State Fair displayed articles from manufacturers, merchants, artists, ladies, and children. Categories at the Utah State Fair six years later also showed the diversity that fairs encouraged: contestants entered samples of home-ground flour and home-grown garden seeds; manufacturers demonstrated a carding machine, cutlery, combs, nails, and blankets. Men sized up a buckskin suit, and their wives evaluated straw hats and bonnets. Necessities, luxuries, and everything in between jumbled together in an unpredictable array.

Camping areas at fairgrounds quickly became focal points for families who wanted to pinch pennies while spending a week at the fair. One of the earliest references to camping at a fair appears in an account of the Maine State Fair in the 1880s: "Many families came and stayed all week, either camping on the grounds or in the row of cottages," a historian wrote, observing that "In those days transportation was by the horse and buggy, the steam cars or the electrics."

Most fairgrounds were located in open countryside, which allowed campers to pick shaded sites under nearby trees. Some campers

**Although fairs were packed with places to eat, lots of families preferred homemade picnics, a tribute to Mom's cooking.** Nebraska State Fair

**Baking and canning remained the staples of a mother's participation. This poster shows that the whole family could have fun by getting involved.** Eastern States Exposition

**This brochure for the Maryland State Fair at Timonium announces "Fun for the entire family"—the goal of fairs for more than a century, and one that most have met with flying colors.** Maryland State Fair

slept on blankets on the ground, or on iron cots in tents. Others slept in canvas-covered wagons. At night, campfires glowed and portable kerosene stoves hissed as families cooked dinner and discussed their busy day.

In 1948 a writer described how to get to the historic campground at the Iowa State Fair: "You turn left when you leave the grandstand and walk past the Midway and the Old Mill and the rollercoaster; past the shuttered dining halls and the lemonade stand." The wooden rollercoaster was gone by 1950, a victim of wartime neglect, but the campground, now covering more than 100 gently rolling acres at the edge of the fairground, continues to host as many as 10,000 campers during a typical fair week. A century ago, campers could spend three days in a 9x12-foot tent, already set up, for $2.

The Iowa fair has always been justly proud of its campground. A 1911 promotional article called it "the finest in the world."

Without assigned spots, campers helped themselves to whatever empty area attracted them on the campground, which was described as "covered with rich blue grass" and "dotted with giant shade trees," including the shellbark hickory, oak, elm, linden, ash, cherry, walnut, butternut, and sycamore.

The campground was particularly busy in 1919, because attendance at that year's "Victory Fair" far exceeded the capacity of Des Moines hotels. In 1927 fair managers announced that the campground was expected to "accommodate the largest crowds that have ever assembled at any one time at any single vacation spot in the state." The campground itself was certainly ready: it had cindered roads and driveways, running water, electric lights, bathrooms, fire and police protection, a grocery store, and a meat market.

The latter facility was handy; stories still circulate about the old days, when campers in farm wag-

ons brought live chickens and butchered them for dinner. One modern camper recalls that his family's first "tent" was a tarp strung over wires. One year they had a little extra money and bought an umbrella tent with a sewn-in floor; a ferocious rainstorm struck the fair that first night, and they stayed dry, imagining what it would have been like under the old tarp. Back then, the campground permitted people to build wooden or cement platforms (since demolished) for their tents. "We bought one of the cement platforms one year and thought that was really living," he recalled.

Longtime camper Virgil McDonnell remembers back to 1931, when he was seven (back then, he observes, the penny arcade actually cost a penny). His family slept in a large, surplus World War I Army tent, which his father had bought for $25. They cooked on a two-burner kerosene stove, and kept their food in an icebox (back then, the name was literal).

McDonnell's father had been a parking lot attendant at the fair since the late 1920s. He remembers that

A girl waits for the cattle judging at the Vermont State Fair in 1941. Thanks to clubs such as the 4-H and FFA, boys and girls found increasing opportunities to take part in the exciting competition at fairs. Jack Delano/Library of Congress, LC-USF-45533-D

Some of the displays staged by manufacturers at fairs aimed at women, some at families, and some, unquestionably, at men, such as this stogie booth at the Utah Territorial Fair in 1892.

"Everybody who was anybody as well as those who were not would come from all the country roundabout, within a radius of 100 miles or more, depending on what and how much they had to exhibit in stock and products. They would come, whole families and clans, with their camping paraphernalia ... tents for all purposes, living room, kitchen and sleeping tents, with old carpets laid on the ground, and stoves, both heating and cooking. The campground was in a grove of scrub oaks, and much of the firewood was oak and it must have been for the smoke of the fires those early autumn days was so blue and odorous, like no other blue or smell of my recollection."

—LAURA MINTO IRWIN, PORTLAND, OREGON, DECEMBER 1939; INTERVIEWED BY SARA WRENN OF THE WPA'S FEDERAL WRITERS PROJECT, PUBLISHED IN *AMERICAN LIFE HISTORIES: MANUSCRIPTS FROM THE FEDERAL WRITERS PROJECT 1936–1940.*

Mr. and Mrs. George Phillips from Colfax, Iowa, enjoy a bite to eat at their state fair's extraordinary campground. The campground is still there, still shady, and still crammed with lucky campers during fair week. Iowa State Fair, Des Moines

The state fair became somewhat of a vacation as more and more folks turned to camping on the grounds as part of the festivities.

This combination guide post and caution reflector signals that the automobile has officially taken over from the horse and buggy as the transportation mode of choice for fairgoers. The Greenbrier Valley Fair became the State Fair of West Virginia. Eamswood Communications, Inc., for the State Fair of West Virginia

some people camped in livestock trucks; they cleaned them out, put down straw to sleep on, and stretched a large piece of canvas over the top. In 1934 he saw a school bus that had been converted into a mobile home. Although, in the 1930s, contemporary accounts referred to the campground as "Tent City," trailers were about to make their appearance. A 1936 article refers to a new "tourist trailer camp." McDonnell saw his first RVs in 1940 or 1941 (the last fair before the war halted the annual event until 1946).

The automobile was already playing a major role in bringing entire families to fairs. Family cars meant more visitors and more exhibits, because it made getting there faster, easier, and cheaper. More people could bring their tents, cots, and stoves, and could stay longer because they could return home more quickly; historians agree that the automobile allowed the fair to truly become a family affair. Day trips became feasible for folks who lived within 100 miles or so. They could rise before sunup, milk the cows and put them in the pasture, leave the family dog to guard the homestead, and set out for a day of fun.

As the fair became more of a family event, an increasing number of women participated in fair activities. A few women, however, had broken the gender barrier long before the time of the baking contest. "Female equestrianism" was a controversial (and popular) early sporting attraction. The first Iowa State Fair, in 1854, awarded a gold watch to the "boldest and most graceful" of 10 female riders. The event generated so much interest that it was repeated the following day. Many other fairs had similar events, usually with only a handful of entrants but with large crowds in the grandstand. During one such display, the ladies rode around the ring single file, then changed horses. The event ended in a sort of race, with one riding bareback.

Complaints entered the official record as early as 1862, when prominent fair officials in several states urged women to stick to purely domestic roles. After two riders were seriously injured in falls at the Minnesota State Fair, newspaper editors harangued their readers about the impropriety of women on horses. The events were scandalous. An Illinois reporter described one show: "Four females actuated by a desire to exhibit themselves to a gaping multitude entered the ring on horseback in order to compete for the ribbons. The contest soon became narrowed down to two, and the contestants, being strong-minded and full of pluck, put their horses upon their speed and gave an exhibition of themselves (one of them especially) such as is rarely seen in so public a place." Afterward, the reporter noted, the fairground "resumed its usual calm and quiet aspect."

In spite of sporadic disapproval, women never retreated from expanding their roles as participants, contestants, and entertainers. They drove race cars as early as 1915, and dove from high towers in thrill shows. One fair staged a boxing match between a man and a woman, prompting a journalist to write, "You might be supposin' they was married, the way the lady hits the gentleman." Women pushed political agendas, erecting "Votes for Women" exhibits. In 1886 the Iowa Woman Suffrage Society had their headquarters in a cottage on the fairground. Eventually, women began staffing commercial booths; by the 1920s, they were demonstrating tractors. Histories of the Ohio State Fair

SEPT.-23-28. INDIANAPOLIS, IND.

Women on horseback—"lady equestrians," as the formal language of the time put it—made some of the first major strides out of the kitchen on behalf of their gender, shown on this 1889 Indiana State Fair poster. They debuted at the Indiana fair back in 1859, when three female riders performed an exhibition. By the 1920s, women were demonstrating tractors. Histories of the Ohio State Fair note that in 1941, that fair got its first female ticket sellers and takers; the men who usually did those jobs were in the military. Indiana State Archives, Commission on Public Records, all rights reserved

"Four females actuated by a desire to exhibit themselves to a gaping multitude entered the ring on horseback in order to compete for the ribbons. The contest soon became narrowed down to two, and the contestants, being strong-minded and full of pluck, put their horses upon their speed and gave an exhibition of themselves (one of them especially) such as is rarely seen in so public a place."

—ILLINOIS REPORTER DESCRIBING EARLY WOMEN'S EQUESTRIAN CONTEST.

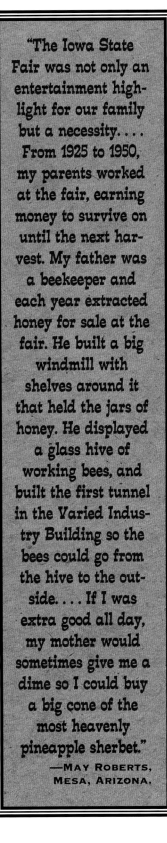

"The Iowa State Fair was not only an entertainment highlight for our family but a necessity. . . . From 1925 to 1950, my parents worked at the fair, earning money to survive on until the next harvest. My father was a beekeeper and each year extracted honey for sale at the fair. He built a big windmill with shelves around it that held the jars of honey. He displayed a glass hive of working bees, and built the first tunnel in the Varied Industry Building so the bees could go from the hive to the outside. . . . If I was extra good all day, my mother would sometimes give me a dime so I could buy a big cone of the most heavenly pineapple sherbet."

—MAY ROBERTS, MESA, ARIZONA.

note that in 1941 the fair got its first female ticket sellers and takers (because so many men were in the military), and that in 1957, the fair's first female livestock judge, 30-year-old Mrs. Maurice Neville, evaluated the Yorkshire swine.

The main opportunities for women at fairs weren't in front of the grandstand but in their own kitchens and workshops during the months before the fairs, creating the items they would enter in what fairs usually called something like the Women's Department of Domestic

Sciences and Arts. In the 1940s, the Minnesota State Fair presented as many as 5,000 exhibits in this department. The allure of the blue ribbon was powerful; some women entered dozens of categories. In a 1953 interview, 71-year-old Christine Arlt of St. Paul described the 100 entries she'd prepared for that year's fair. She'd begun entering in 1919, and had collected nearly a thousand blue ribbons to date.

Baking was the premier category, and a woman's ability to produce excellent cakes and pies possessed a

symbolic importance far beyond the caloric value of dessert. When a popular song asked, "Can she bake a cherry pie?" the talent implied a host of related domestic skills that husbands found invaluable. Judges (who skipped breakfast, and dipped their fingers in ice water to make them more sensitive to texture and consistency) were readily available to evaluate the cakes that a 1903 writer called "monuments to housewifery—chocolate-layer and cocoanut, marble, mountain, sponge and snow, angel-food and jelly-twist."

It was a tough job, but someone had to do it. Watching a boy watching the judges, a writer in the early 1940s once imagined him temporarily abandoning his dreams of becoming a policeman or an auto mechanic as he asked his mother, "Gee, who do you suppose tastes all those cakes and pies?"

At New Jersey's Great Inter-State Fair in 1893, entrants competed with 10 kinds of bread, including bran, graham, cornbread, rye, wheat, raised biscuits, and rusk. Forty-four kinds of cake were also open for entries.

Along with baked goods, the slate of categories at a county fair would include many kinds of candy, jelly and

**The patriotic overtones of this display by the Girls Canning Club at a fair in Bibb County, Georgia, signal that World War I was still raging in Europe. The poster at right says, "Save fat for the soldiers."**
Georgia Department of Archives and History

"Monuments to housewifery—chocolate-layer and cocoanut, marble, mountain, sponge and snow, angel-food and jelly-twist."
—WRITER APPRAISING BAKED GOODS CONTEST, 1903.

**Members of 4-H clubs flocked to the competition at fairs across the country, particularly in the Midwest. This girl wears her club jacket at the 1966 Oklahoma State Fair.** State Fair of Oklahoma

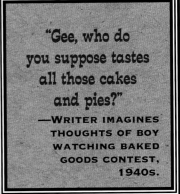

"Gee, who do you suppose tastes all those cakes and pies?"
—WRITER IMAGINES THOUGHTS OF BOY WATCHING BAKED GOODS CONTEST, 1940s.

preserves, pickles, and mountains of canned fruit and vegetables. There might be sorghum molasses in jugs or tubs of cottage cheese. The Iowa State Fair in the mid-1930s offered 900 prizes in the domestic arena, awarding ribbons for a dozen kinds of bread and rolls, 15 types of layer cake, popcorn balls, sun-dried fruits, cheese straws, Saratoga chips (an early name for potato chips) and catsup.

Although most winners were content with neighborhood bragging rights, a few were destined for greatness on a larger stage. A notable entrant to the first state fair in Texas, the Lone Star Fair of 1852, was Gail Borden, Jr., who would later make his processed, condensed milk into a national brand. His fame and success were still in the future; this time, Borden entered a dried "meat biscuit."

Clothing was another common category in the days before "store-bought" became a routine rather than a treat. At the Illinois State Fair in 1861, ladies won prizes for homemade hoop skirts, bonnets of velvet or straw, and woven stockings. Fairs often handed out ribbons for embroidery and knitting (the Indiana State Fair in 1872 awarded premiums for knit corsets and knit drawers). Four years later, the fair offered a prize for the best crocheted opera hood, about as non-agrarian a necessity as can be imagined.

As early as 1855, housewives at the Illinois fair were, according to one account, "excited over demonstrations of the sewing machine," which had been patented a few years earlier. A woman complained that the device would lead to people buying store-bought clothes, now that they could be so cheaply made, thus destroying an important domestic skill. But few women were opposed to any device that helped them get more done in a day. A typical 1930 display of Singer sewing machines included both the machines themselves and dresses that had been sewn on them, with placards listing the price of the dress pattern and the material, compared to the cost of a ready-made garment. Soon, fairs included specific categories for machine sewing, for such items as sunbonnets and kitchen aprons, and for hand

Judges tie a first-prize ribbon on canned vegetables entered by Mrs. Frank Metzger of Indianapolis. The judges (from left) are Mrs. Lloyd Cutler of Crown Point, Mrs. Harry Stevenson of Bloomington (in charge of the culinary department at the fair), and Mrs. Fred Ebert of Lowell, the fair's assistant superintendent.
J. C. Allen and Son, Inc.

This page from the entry guide for the 1916 Durham Fair shows that first prize for cakes was higher than first prize for bread—a reasonable policy.
Durham Agricultural Fair Association, Inc.

sides, fairgoers saw dulcimers, metal coffins, and stuffed birds. At the Indiana State Fair in 1872, a company displayed false teeth that a small machine moved up and down in a chewing motion. For families interested in home entertainment, there would be a display of pianos (grand, semi-grand, square, and upright models), church and parlor organs, and melodeons. Practical gadgets for the home included rat traps, hedge trimmers, and knife sharpeners.

By the late 1940s, while the men were checking out rototillers and insulation, their wives were eyeing canning jars and vacuum cleaners ("Hear how quiet it is," one sign read). Another sign announced, with midway-style exuberance, the "First Showing of the Meadows Press Ironer, the Most Remarkable Household Appliance of All Time." This machine ran on electricity, as well as natural gas and gasoline for those who hadn't yet received rural electrification.

sewing (sample categories included camisoles and darned hose).

Opera hoods were a rarity. More realistically, one fair rewarded thrift with a prize for the best boy's suit made from cast-off garments. Making things cheaply was always an important aspect of home crafts. The opposite of opera hoods resulted from a 1951 advertising promotion at the Texas State Fair, when the Textile Bag Association handed out hundreds of thousands of booklets that taught women how to make clothes out of feed and flour sacks.

Other categories in the domestic-arts division form an evocative list of vanished skills and crafts: brooms, laundry soap, and corn-shuck mattresses. Prizes were awarded for tallow candles, castor oil, and linseed oil. Underlining the self-sufficient nature of farms, one category was for a collection of six or more varieties of garden seed.

Fairs also broadened attendance by expanding the large exhibitions of inventions and machinery to include products that appealed to a greater diversity of the public. Aiming at female consumers, a fair in the 1860s offered prizes for the most effective washing machine that rubbed clothes between two wooden surfaces. Rubber nipples (1872) and vegetable slicers (1886)—obviously aimed at a feminine audience—appeared as well. Strolling the elaborate, decorated displays, which often featured carpets on the floor and potted plants at the

At the 1946 Indiana State Fair, a 4-H member from Marion County exhibited the results of her study comparing the old way to wash laundry with a new electric washing machine. Based on washing once a week per year, the old way took a total of 17 days; the housewife had to pump 3,380 gallons of water by hand, thereby lifting 31 tons of water and clothing. The electric machine reduced the amount of time spent to 11 days; since it pumped the water itself, the total weight hoisted by the hard-working housewife was down to an easy 1.4 tons.

In the mid-1870s, an intriguing new device called a typewriter had drawn curious onlookers who watched displays of a machine that produced capital letters. By 1878 it made lowercase letters as well. The telephone was another popular attraction with both husbands and wives, and was demonstrated at fairs two years after its invention in 1875.

Fairs were natural venues to demonstrate broadcast media to large, eager audiences. Live radio broadcasts from fairgrounds began in the late 1920s. A decade later, experimental televisions began to appear. At the Indiana State Fair in 1939, nearly 40,000 people paid a dime to see a television display. Television did not find a receptive audience at first. In 1948 the Indiana fair board wanted to keep television manufacturers out of the exhibition hall, because nobody could pick up a station from their home, and unscrupulous salesmen might sell sets without telling

people about the minor inconvenience of not being able to find anything to watch. A year later, the fair board rejected television coverage of fair events, arguing that if harness races were televised, people wouldn't pay to see the races in person, especially if it was hot or rainy.

To expand attendance, fair organizers even got babies into the act. Baby contests were a staple at fairs as early as the 1890s, when the Illinois State Fair offered awards in more than two dozen categories, including the heaviest, lightest, and prettiest infant. The Minnesota State Fair in 1915 pitted city babies against country babies, and Minneapolis infants against those from St. Paul. The Louisiana State Fair drew 1,060 diapered contestants at a "Better Baby" contest in 1926.

In the days when store-bought clothes were an extravagance for farmers, needlework was a necessity. These county champions gathered at the Montana State Fair in 1913. Margurite Henderson (later Mrs. John Higginson) of Jordon, Montana, is fourth from the left in the second row. This photo was made by R. H. McKay of Missoula. Montana Historical Society, Helena

Sewing machines may seem to be an innocuous and common product, here displayed at the 1966 Oklahoma State Fair, but when they were introduced, they generated controversy. Some conservative women thought that the machines would destroy the art of hand-sewing and encourage store-bought clothes, apparently considered a needless extravagance. State Fair of Oklahoma

145

## "First Showing of the Meadows Press Ironer, the Most Remarkable Household Appliance of All Time."

—FAIRGROUND PLACARD OF 1940s.

"Every woman has a right to be free from the slavery of old-time hand irons," one of the signs says. "This is the Wonder age." This display is flanked by booths for Shredded Wheat and Kerr canning jars. The photo was made in 1927; Bass Photo Co. was the Indiana fair's official photographer for a number of years.

R.H.McKay 1913

Some of these events were formidably serious. At the Indiana State Fair in 1920, for example, the men and women who judged the infants were supervised by Dr. Ada Schweitzer of the State Board of Health's child hygiene division. The infants were scrutinized and graded for 123 possible defects, enough to give any once-proud mother the willies. Judges awarded points for "a mother free from overwork or worry" and "gentle play with quiet laughter." Points were deducted if the baby wasn't protected from "kissers with germs, fingers poking for teeth, showing off, bounding and high tossing." Also on the prohibited list were pacifiers, dirt, discord, loud voices, and those classic scourges of childhood—nagging and jazz.

Once these toddlers grew up, promoters of fairs began dreaming up ways to keep them coming back. Fairs had always educated adults: by the 1930s, large

Baby contests became exceptionally popular when population growth was the order of the day in pioneer communities. Some of these frontier mothers donned flamboyant hats for their big day at the fair. If crying triggered demerits, the tot at front left center had just fallen out of the running. This photo was taken in 1913 by R. H. McKay of Missoula.

fairs in the Midwest were featuring lectures by professors, social workers, and other sorts of experts on topics that ranged from interior decoration and weaving to child psychology and farm plumbing. Educational displays at the Indiana State Fair during the 1930s included banners that declared "Stamp Out Diphtheria!" and "Tuberculosis Can Be Prevented!" At a Purdue University exhibit, farmers learned how to kill weeds with sodium chlorate and discovered how electric lights could increase egg production during the winter.

Fairs began concentrating on teaching lessons to school-aged children, as well. The Illinois State Fair was one of the earliest architects of such programs; in 1899 the fair established a Home Economics School for Girls, aged 16 and up. Similar features gradually became widespread for both boys and girls.

Fairs created a rapidly expanding slate of contest categories for children, tailored to local conditions. In the 1930s, the Arizona State Fair included entries from both public schools and Indian schools among the displays

**Club members examine an educational booth at the Nebraska State Fair. Most fairs blended educational exhibits with commercial displays.** Nebraska State Fair

Question: "What do you think of the animals at the livestock exhibit?" Answer: "I think they stink."
—INTERVIEW WITH THE CHILD KING AT KIDS DAY, CALIFORNIA'S SANTA CLARA COUNTY FAIR.

Deciding where to go first demanded real teamwork at the busy fairground. This happy band of sisters was about to explore the 1941 Vermont State Fair. Jack Delano/Library of Congress, LC-USF-35-54

Mrs. Lew Shanks of Indianapolis presents the winner's cup to Homer G. Keesler of New Ross, Indiana. Homer won the Kiddies' Circus and Pet Parade competition, with a wagon pulled by his dog "Bob."
J. C. Allen and Son, Inc.

created by children's clubs. At the Minnesota State Fair in 1921, Boy Scouts exhibited their skills at map-making, knot-tying, signaling, and first aid. They cooked doughnuts and built towers. Forty years later, at the Oregon State Fair, 4-H contests included electricity, entomology, beekeeping, forestry, photography, woodworking, and wool making.

Fairs also sponsored special contests for kids, including bicycle races and track meets. The Indiana state government tried out a sure-fire ploy in 1934 by declaring that Wednesday, September 5, was "Education Day" at the state fair; all students who attended the fair would be excused from school that day—not a very hard decision, one would expect.

Publicizing the fact that children enjoyed visiting the fair, California's Santa Clara County Fair chose a boy and a girl as king and queen for the day on Kid's Day. Manager Russell Pettit looked for children who were photogenic and unafraid of a microphone. One year he verified that kids do say the darndest things. During an impromptu radio interview, the master of ceremonies asked the Kid King how he liked the animals in the livestock exhibit. "I think they stink," said the King. Thinking quickly, the host switched topics and asked what he thought of the chickens. The boy replied, with perfect candor, "They make an awful mess"—about as much of a mess as he had just made of the interview.

All the kids and parents at the fair had to eat. This need was among the easiest to satisfy. A visitor to a large state fair in 1921 strolled up to the information booth and asked where the officers of the fair ate their meals. When the booth attendant said it would be easier to find the officers at the administration building, the visitor replied that he didn't want to talk to them, he just wanted to find a good spot to eat lunch. He figured that the guys who ran the show would know where to find the best chow.

Actually, no spot was best. According to one's appetite and diet, fairs had dozens. Places run by local churches or women's clubs offered full meals, luring passers-by with the aromas of roast beef, grilled pork, and fried chicken. For snacks and desserts, fairgrounds have always been free-for-alls of savory, sweet, high-calorie goodies: buttered white popcorn (once a novelty, now a staple), huge crocks of pink lemonade, cold bottles of orange drink, and sticky sheaves of green cotton candy.

Hungry fairgoers develop their own traditions, returning year after year to places such as the lunch counter run by Ida "Ma" Johnson, a hallmark at the Minnesota fair from 1910 into the 1940s. The large

**Although most kids were spectators at fairs, they were occasionally enlisted for publicity purposes, as in this photo from the 1930s.** California State Fair

sign on her wall—"If your wife can't cook, keep her for a pet and eat here"—was always good for a laugh. Interviewed late in her career, she recalled that when she had started her lunch counter, eggs had cost 12¢ a dozen, and sandwich buns arrived in barrels that held 30 dozen and cost $2.40.

Always, servings were plentiful and the grub was honest. At the turn of the century, a 35¢ roast chicken dinner included pie, cheese, and ice cream, washed down with coffee or milk. In the 1920s, you could eat your fill for 50¢; one entrepreneur sent the food around the banquet-style table on tiny flat cars that rolled on a track in the middle of the table.

Less formal meals could be had at open-air grills, where the hot dogs sizzled and the onions sputtered.

**African-American children look through the fence at a fair in Greensboro, Georgia, October 1941. White school children were admitted free one day, and African-American school children the following day. As always, the Ferris wheel in the background offered an attraction that was visible far and wide.** Jack Delano/Library of Congress, LC-USF33-21216-M2

"If your wife can't cook, keep her for a pet and eat here."
—SIGN IN IDA "MA" JOHNSON'S LUNCH COUNTER, AT THE MINNESOTA FAIR 1910–1940s.

The hamburger stand at the Minnesota State Fair, 1917. Apparently, cigars were considered part of a balanced meal back then. The fresh buttermilk would be unusual at modern fairs.
Minnesota Historical Society

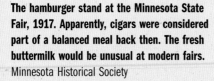

Outsized hamburgers were once a great novelty, and vendors competed to offer the largest ones, calling them "jumbo," "king-size," "mountain size," and "huge."

And everyone had room for the occasional sweet. Once, taffy was the lodestone that drew adults and kids alike. One author vividly remembered the taffy at his local fair, grandly known as "Elgin honeycomb cream chewing candy." When he was young, he figured that this candy was the main reason for having the fair. Candy makers worked in full view. Metal hooks pulled the thick, shiny loops of taffy in a sinuous dance. When it was white, the candy seller snipped off pieces with a large pair of shears, delivering it still warm to the buyer's hand.

In Indiana, the prime purveyor was Caroline Jessop, who operated a candy stand under the banner "Mrs. C.

**Several Midwestern fairs in dairy states offered all-you-can-drink milk stands, and there were always plenty of thirsty milk-lovers around to make sure the proprietors lost money. Rose Laubhan of Saginaw, Michigan, recalls one such concession at the Minnesota State Fair in the 1950s: "My brother and I usually went to the milk stand the first thing," she says. "We could drink all the milk we wanted for 10 cents and nearly sloshed when we walked away. The milk was cold and delicious."**
Photo by Minneapolis Journal, Minnesota Historical Society

"We loved the 'Wolf Brand Chili' booth. You could smell that spicy delicious stuff all over the fairgrounds. They also gave away free samples every day with crackers. Just over the way was the Dr. Pepper booth giving away free Dr. Pepper and Seven-Up. We lived it up."

—BONNIE FIELDS, BLOOMING GROVE, TEXAS, REMEMBERING THE NAVARRO COUNTY FAIR IN THE 1930S AND 1940S.

The original caption for this photo, recorded by photographer John Allen, read, "Ready, ready, and they're all red hot, a pickle in the middle and an onion on top!" He took this photo at the Indiana State Fair, September 1930. J. C. Allen and Son, Inc.

Jessop, the Lady Confectioner." She and her husband had started out by hauling her candy-making machinery from fair to fair in the 1850s. She devised her own recipes and flavorings. Later, her operation grew large enough to require two trucks, several cars, a crew of workers and various family members. During World War II, the Jessops were the only ones with candy at the fairgrounds. Mrs. Jessop died in 1916, and the then-famous brand of taffy and "Jessop's Butterscotch Corn" passed into the hands of her children. They had always bought corn from the same supplier until a grandson started growing his own. Today, the fifth generation runs the business, and the taffy is sold at five state fairs and many county fairs.

A veteran concessionaire, interviewed in the

early 1920s, revealed the secret of his considerable success at selling lemonade: "We feed 'em, then we water 'em," he said. Catering to the crowds in the grandstand, he dispatched his crew to sell peanuts and popcorn first. Sometimes they'd toss out handfuls of peanuts to the crowd; many of the people who caught a peanut found that they couldn't eat just one. The lemonade came next, and the vendors methodically marched all the way down from the top of the grandstand to the front rows, clinking the cold bottles as they went, and ignoring everyone until they got down to the front. That way, all of the parched people in the crowd had to watch others getting their drinks first, a sight that made them thirstier and thirstier.

Jessop's caramel corn is still sold at the Indiana State Fair; the confection advertised here, however, was taffy. Shown are Uncle Ed Jessop (left); Orin Morgan of Macon, Georgia (center); Grandma Jessop (second from right), who founded the family business with her husband; and Uncle Joseph Jessop (right).
Indiana State Fair

# After the Fair

In central Virginia, at the site of what used to be an annual county fair, all signs of the ancient festivities are gone. The fairground has returned to pasture. But if you fly over in a small aircraft, you can still see a circular depression in the ground where, for 20 years, horses raced during fair time. Human memory is equally indelible.

Fairs provided intense experiences in a time when novelties and thrills were rare. In the months and weeks before fair week, excitement inexorably built. The plodding wagon ride over dirt roads was excruciating, as were later traffic jams or crowded trolley car rides that stopped too often. Standing in a long line at the gate was sheer torture. But once the gate opened, the wait was instantly forgotten.

Inside, there was always something new and familiar, a complex eddy in the rushing river of time, a confluence of modernity and tradition. For every new food fad, every Greek gyro or skewer of Japanese teriyaki chicken, there was a humble corn dog and a sugar-frosted elephant ear.

And always the memories are strong, pungent, and vivid after decades have passed. Jubilation, disappointment, adrenaline, and titillation. Millions of fairgoers with 100 memories apiece. It is amazing what sticks in the mind. The office staff at a northern fair once received a letter containing 50¢, along with a note from an 85-year-old man who said that his conscience had been bothering him, and he needed to settle accounts. When he was a boy, he had once sneaked into the fair by crawling under the fence. It was a common ploy: one boy dug a hole, word spread, and other kids crawled under until guards found the hole and filled it. But whenever one filthy boy saw another at the fair, they both knew why.

Going to the fair, showing animals, entering food or craft competitions, prowling the midway—all these things become family traditions, part of the linkage between generations. A longtime fairgoer from Mississippi once recalled that when her son served an Army tour in England, he took his annual leave not at Christmastime, but during fair week, which was much more fun.

It seemed a shame that the fair ever had to end. Strolling back to his hotel in 1920, a fairgoer reflected on "that disintegration of the holiday impulse which was filling the streets of the town with human particles, weary in body and brain, disheveled, draggled, dusty, often censorious and sometimes cross. Holidays will end so, for so they have ended from the beginning of time, and it is for Time, who is so wise in such matters, to arrange a perspective in which, by next summer, last fall's fair shall be all enchantment again."

> "There is the moment after clicking through the turnstile at the fairgrounds gate when the crowds milling around in the heat and the dust, the many sounds and smells, make the State Fair a fabulous and mythical city, beyond actual experience. . . ."
> —DONALD GRANT, WRITING IN THE CHRISTIAN SCIENCE MONITOR, 1937.

**The sun sets over the Iowa fairground, but the fun continues into the night.** Iowa State Fair, Des Moines

# Carnese

## THE LANGUAGE OF THE MIDWAY

**agent:** A carnie who runs a crooked game on the midway. As a veteran explained in a confessional article written in 1949, "the agent has to have a lot of guts, a fast tongue, and a good knowledge of human nature."

**bally:** From "ballyhoo." To spiel in front of a sideshow. "Barkers" work for shows, and "grinders" spiel for concessions.

**barnyard golf:** Horseshoes. *Time* magazine, in the Sept. 9, 1935, issue, reported that the barnyard golf champion at the Iowa State Fair that year was from California.

***Billboard:*** The "bible" of the carnival trade. The long-running tabloid has also been described as "the carnies' Bhagavad Gita and mail address, too." In a 1942 article in the *New Yorker*, Fred Smythe, manager of the Ringling Brothers and Barnum & Bailey sideshow, said that he advertised in *Billboard* in the summer issues for freaks for the following season.

**butcher:** A vendor or hawker. The word appears in a 1953 magazine article describing the fact that barkers invariably announced that a pending show would start in exactly 4 minutes, hurrying people in, when in fact the show might not start for 15 or 20 minutes. The audience was then stuck, "sitting in a hot, half-empty tent, a captive audience to the dreary spiel of a candy butcher."

**carnese:** The jargon-filled, opaque language of carnival workers. In an article entitled "Mysteries of the Carnival Language," published in *American Mercury* magazine in 1935, author C. Wolverton defined this as "a deliberately disguised speech. Few professions preserve the intimate arcana of their trade more jealously than carnival men," he observed, "because no calling could suffer more from public knowledge of its details than theirs."

**cooch:** Most etymologists agree that the word derived from "hoochie-coochie," only to admit they don't know the origin of that term. One reference says that cooch was "an early form of belly dance," and was being performed at Coney Island in the 1890s. An article from the early 1900s called cooch "the fuzzy-wuzzy dance" or "the wollopy-wollop." In the 1920s, cooch performed to jazz was sometimes called the "shimmy." Burlesque pioneer Irving Zeidman described this version as a "demonic, orgiastic spectacle . . . The girls would sprawl out on the runway, twist, writhe, squirm and shake, each to her own inventive obscene devices."

**cutting up a jack pot:** Gossiping.

**fairbank:** Persuading a customer to increase the stakes successively on each play.

**Fatima:** Generic name for an exotic dancer; used when the sideshow operator couldn't reasonably claim that the dancer was Little Egypt.

**First Ride:** The merry-go-round, referring to the fact that it was the oldest of all midway mechanical amusements.

**flash:** Impressive prizes used for decoration (they are rarely won by customers).

**flatties:** Dishonest concessionaires.

**floss candy:** Cotton candy.

**forty-milers:** A term for carnivals that travel by trailer and make short trips between stops. A second meaning (along with the term **first-of-Mayers**) was unseasoned, nonprofessional carnival workers who drop out of the carnie biz early in the season.

**front end:** Concessions, games of chance; as opposed to the "back end," the sideshows.

**G-top:** Carnival tent for gambling by the agents themselves.

**gaff:** The apparatus for controlling a game. On a skillo wheel, a mechanism enabled the operator to lower the metal collar on the spinning arrow, which rubbed against the brass collar on the arrow's axle, thus braking the arrow.

**gilly:** A show that moves by truck, as opposed to train. A *Life* magazine article in 1940 described the Buckeye State Shows as a "gilly" show; it filled 28 trucks, along with various cars and trailers. As a verb, in some usages, to "gilly" a show meant to move it from the railroad to the grounds where it would be set up.

**given Brown's cow:** A performance cut short in order to pack in more customers, when business is good.

**grab joint:** Originally, a hamburger stand, then any stand that sells such things as sandwiches, ice cream, and cotton candy.

**grind stores:** Games where the customer had no chance.

**grinding:** For a barker or spieler, continuously repeating a few sentences.

**hanky-panks:** Oddly, this term meant honest games. Even these games make profits, because the cheap prizes they give away are never worth the price of a play.

**"Hey Rube!":** Carnie distress call, triggers a free-for-all.

**hoosier:** A hick, someone from the country.

**hot spot:** Location where 80 or 90 percent of the people who attend the fair must pass.

**human curiosities:** Synonym for "freak," a term that many members of this peculiar group disliked. They preferred terms such as "human oddities" or "strange people."

Since this talker has a microphone, he isn't leather-lunging it, a term from the days when volume was self-generated. His expressive gestures, however, are a timeless part of the art of pulling in a crowd. This photo was made at the Vermont State Fair in 1941. Library of Congress

another previous town, so the Gratz police sent them packing immediately.

**mortgage lifters:** 1950s-era Iowa slang for hogs, because they were so profitable.

**mud:** Plaster figurines; a cheap prize.

**patch:** A fixer or legal adjuster, who bribes the local officials and cops in advance so that they won't interfere with the plucking of rubes. Writing in the *Christian Science Monitor* in July 1947, John Paul Jones observed, "The day of the 'patch man,' whose job was to pay off the local police, has passed."

**pie car:** Where circus employees gamble at night after the circus is over.

**pig iron:** Midway rides, such as the Ferris wheel, carousel, and Whip.

**pleasure wheel:** 1890's name for early Ferris wheels.

**punk day:** Children's day.

**red-lighting:** Referring to shows that moved by rail, a way to get rid of carnies who caused too much trouble; they were tossed off the train once it was well out of town and up to speed.

**shill:** Someone who buys a ticket at a sideshow right after the bally, to encourage the crowd. Also, people who pretend to be bystanders and urge on gamblers; also called cappers, sticks, and pluggers.

**ironclad:** Describes a town where the carnies enjoyed police protection.

**joint:** A gambling tent.

**kid show:** Freak show, also known as a "ten-in-one."

**leather-lung:** To bark or spiel. As James Poling wrote in the *Saturday Evening Post* on April 11, 1953, the term describes the work of the old "talkers" and "grinders" who "relied solely on their vocal cords. But with the introduction of the microphone and the tape recorder and the loudspeaker, the old-timers assure you, things began to deteriorate." A barker named "Duke" Jeanette, with the James Strates carnival in the '50s, told Poling, "When we used to leather-lung it we had some very great orators. Now, these youngsters are helpless without a mike."

**lumber:** Seats at a show, as in a grandstand.

**mark:** The chump who wastes his money on crooked games. Also known as a fall guy, rube, simp (short for "simpleton") or come-on.

**mit** (or **mitt**) **camp**, also **mittcamp:** Where gypsies tell fortunes. A *Time* magazine article from Sept. 29, 1958, mentioned some "palm-reading and pocket-picking gypsies" in connection with a mittcamp. During the week before the fair in Gratz, Pennsylvania, gypsies had stolen some pigs at

**silo:** A motordrome.

**skillo:** A concession.

**skin game, skin stuff:** Crooked games on the midway.

**slum:** Cheap prizes.

**splasher:** On a motion ride, someone who vomits.

**stick:** Someone who plays for the house and appears to win large amounts, to attract chumps.

**strong game:** A game that is rigged to pay a high percentage to the operator. Operating such a game was called "working strong."

**thief:** Agent of a "strong" concession.

**tip:** The crowd or audience.

**tossing the broads:** Three-card monte, probably referring to playing it with queen face cards.

**turn:** A signal for ticket-sellers to go to work.

**whiz mobs:** Pickpockets. A favorite ploy would be to have the barker warn everyone that pickpockets were in the crowd and to be careful. Lots of people would subconsciously pat their wallets, telling the pickpockets exactly where they were carrying their money.

**worms:** The snakes used by snake handlers in midway shows.

Ever interested in progress and symbolic modernity, a few fairs installed monorails, such as this one at the Oklahoma fairground in the late 1960s—a sure sign of times a-changing. State Fair of Oklahoma

Ribbons for pears, peaches, butter beans, and pickles are included in this quilt, displayed at the 1929 Indiana State Fair. There's no such thing as too many, according to one longtime participant; she has a "whole wall full" at home, but is always intent on winning one more. Indiana State Archives, Indiana Commission on Public Records, all rights reserved

"People came from all over this part of the state for the fair. It was all kicked off by a big parade through downtown Blooming Grove. . . . I always rode my horse and carried the flag. That was so important to me. One year I was the 'Sweetheart' and I thought that was the best thing that could ever happen to me. Of course I was 14 and it was a big deal back then."

—BONNIE FIELDS, BLOOMING GROVE, TEXAS, RECALLING THE NAVARRO COUNTY FAIR OF THE 1930S AND 1940S.

BIRD'S-EYE VIEW EASTERN STATES EXPOSITION, WEST SPRINGFIELD, MASS.

The Eastern States Exposition in West Springfield, Massachusetts, was founded in 1916, and is unique in having the full participation of several states (Massachusetts, Connecticut, Vermont, Maine, Rhode Island, and New Hampshire). In 1936, the river shown at top inundated the fairground. The large building at center is the Coliseum, begun in 1916.

The banner in the background advertises more substantial food, but, given the choice, kids will opt for spun sugar every time.
J. C. Allen and Son, Inc.

# Fairbanking a Chump

"'So this mark walks up to the joint and I screw the sticks. I keep on grinding. He wants to play and he's plenty lush. He stirs the skillo and I let him win a cuter. Then I jackpot him. Is he in a heat?! I'm working the gaff, and splitting the nails, I'm that good. I keep on fairbanking the chump until he is between a poop and a sweat. The score is half a C and he's broke. Do you know what this mark does then? His knees fold up and he's sitting on his keester in front of the joint with his kisser rubbed up against the bally cloth.'

"This is substantially a word-for-word report of a colloquy by one of the smoothest workers I have ever known. The essence of his recitation follows: A customer comes up to Red's concession. Red tells his outside workers to leave. The man is prosperous. He wants to play. Red lets him win a quarter, then gives his customer a chance to increase his winnings (or so the customer thinks). Red is in fine fettle, and can stop the arrow at any space he wishes. The customer is induced to play at increasingly larger stakes. He loses $50 and is broke. The customer faints and sinks to the ground, his face pressing against the canvas."

—FROM "MYSTERIES OF THE CARNIVAL LANGUAGE," C. WOLVERTON, AMERICAN MERCURY, 1935.

"One of the best memories of my young life was the trip to the state fair. I was reared in southwest Alabama in a small rural town and the fair was in the 'big city' of Birmingham. . . . One man in town owned an older school bus and he took a bus load every year. We left at 4 a.m. and we slept some on the ride, but mostly we were too excited to sleep. My brother was three years younger and I can remember my mom saying it was the only day of the year except Christmas when she did not need to call us more than once to get up."
—PATRICIA BREWER, CLANTON, ALABAMA, AT THE ALABAMA STATE FAIR IN THE 1940S.

"...and it is for Time, who is so wise in such matters, to arrange a perspective in which, by next summer, last fall's fair shall be all enchantment again."
—REFLECTIONS OF A FAIRGOER RETURNING TO HIS HOTEL, 1920s.

# INDEX